Afrikinesis

This book provides scholars and non-specialists alike with a roadmap for effectively conducting culturally aware, historically relevant research on African dance and on any dance style that contains African elements.

This book explains why Western research paradigms are inadequate for research on Africana dance. It exposes the value of utilizing an appropriate research paradigm that offers researchers a broader perspective and a transparent, unfettered process for analysis in under-researched topics such as African and African diaspora dance styles. Researchers are introduced to the African dance aesthetic, characteristically African body movements, definitions of steps, understandings within African culture, and a host of other jewels that facilitate a deeper grasp on the subject and refine the quality of the scholar's research, its findings, and its proficiency.

This book will be of great interest to scholars of African dance studies.

Ofosuwa M. Abiola, Ph.D., is Associate Professor of Africana Dance History and Associate Dean of Research and Creative Endeavors at Howard University.

Routledge Advances in Theatre & Performance Studies

This series is our home for cutting-edge, upper-level scholarly studies and edited collections. Considering theatre and performance alongside topics such as religion, politics, gender, race, ecology, and the avant-garde, titles are characterized by dynamic interventions into established subjects and innovative studies on emerging topics.

Boundaries of Violence in Early Modern England
Samantha Dressel and Matthew Carter

Bourdieu in the Studio
Decolonising and Decentering Actor Training through Ludic Activism
Evi Stamatiou

Ethical Agility in Dance
Rethinking Technique in British Contemporary Dance
Noyale Colin, Catherine Seago, Kathryn Stamp

At the Threshold
Contemporary Theatre, Art, and Music of Iran
Rana Esfandiary

Gut Knowledges
Culinary Performance and Activism in the Post-Truth Era
Kristin Hunt

Butoh, as Heard by a Dancer
Dominique Savitri Bonarjee

For more information about this series, please visit: www.routledge.com/Routledge-Advances-in-Theatre-Performance-Studies/book-series/RATPS

Afrikinesis
A Paradigm for Research on African and African Diaspora Dance

Ofosuwa M. Abiola

LONDON AND NEW YORK

First published 2024
by Routledge
4 Park Square, Milton Park, Abingdon, Oxon OX14 4RN

and by Routledge
605 Third Avenue, New York, NY 10158

Routledge is an imprint of the Taylor & Francis Group, an informa business

© 2024 Ofosuwa M. Abiola

The right of Ofosuwa M. Abiola to be identified as author of this work has been asserted in accordance with sections 77 and 78 of the Copyright, Designs and Patents Act 1988.

All rights reserved. No part of this book may be reprinted or reproduced or utilised in any form or by any electronic, mechanical, or other means, now known or hereafter invented, including photocopying and recording, or in any information storage or retrieval system, without permission in writing from the publishers.

Trademark notice: Product or corporate names may be trademarks or registered trademarks, and are used only for identification and explanation without intent to infringe.

British Library Cataloguing-in-Publication Data
A catalogue record for this book is available from the British Library

ISBN: 978-1-032-61195-2 (hbk)
ISBN: 978-1-032-61196-9 (pbk)
ISBN: 978-1-003-46249-1 (ebk)

DOI: 10.4324/9781003462491

Typeset in Times New Roman
by Apex CoVantage, LLC

For the Creator
For Araku, Ayinde, and Tchesar

Contents

	List of Illustrations	*viii*
	Acknowledgments	*ix*
	Preface	*x*
1	Performative practices and documentation through an African lens: An introduction	1
2	Overview of African culture and its reflection on dance	11
3	Identifying African dance body movements	18
4	Application of the Afrikinesis paradigm	29
5	A synergistic union: Afrikinesis and African dance research	41
	Appendix	*45*
	Quick reference glossary	*48*
	Bibliography	*53*
	Index	*57*

Illustrations

Charts

3.1	Torso Angles	20

Figures

3.2	Low Torso	21
3.3	High Torso	22
3.4	Medium Torso	23

Acknowledgments

I would like to thank my sons, Araku and Ayinde, and my mother, Tchesar, for their unwavering support and love as I ventured on this project and every project I undertake. To my mentees, Truly Davis and Rikiesha Metzger, who unwittingly showed me the value of the African dance research methodology delineated in this book, I am eternally grateful. Without witnessing their application of this framework into their research on African diaspora dance and African diaspora arts in general, I would not have thought to name, articulate, and expand this work into an official paradigm.

Preface

As I embarked upon writing my first book, my concern was to make and substantiate the argument that African dance systems could be used as primary sources and as a methodology for constructing historical accounts of events in Africa.[1] As a graduate student conducting research on African dance systems, in countless research scenarios, I was continually confronted with the rhetoric that primary, African-derived sources for constructing African historical accounts were scarce, if not nonexistent. This stance was unacceptable to me. I had performed African dances all my life since I was five years old. As an adult, I taught African dance and founded an African dance company that I operated for 15 years, and I trained the company members in Africa and America. The dances were incredibly rich with historical content. These actions prompted my "eureka" moment. The history, societal values, historic and current culture, and newly emerging cultural developments were all embedded in the traditional dances. Thus, the emphasis of my first book was on teaching researchers how to extract the information from the dances. At the time, and not until recently, it did not occur to me that the structure of African dances could be used as a road map, a template, for research on African dance.

Over the past couple of years, I noticed my graduate students referencing my work in their dissertations, theses, and theories about dance, but their studies were not on traditional African dance per se. Some of their research concerned dance styles that were not commonly associated with African dance. My graduate students' work spanned diverse genres of dance, and in addition to historic dance systems, they included contemporary dance styles. Not only did the African dance positions, movement vocabulary, etc., that were delineated in my book on authentic African dances facilitate understanding of my graduate students' arguments, but they were also extremely relevant. I had to take a closer look at what I may have serendipitously stumbled across in my earlier work. This handbook, *Afrikinesis: A Paradigm for Research on African and African Diaspora Dance*, is the result of that closer look. I named the paradigm "Afrikinesis," because the term simultaneously signifies body movement and the progenitors of such body movements – Africans.

The dance systems, body movements, steps, and movement vocabulary described in this work are by no means exhaustive. It is impossible to witness and therefore describe each and every step ever executed on the continent of Africa. As such, this work is meant to be a guide. It seeks to guide the researcher in their endeavors to recognize and understand African dance steps and African body movements when witnessed and to organize a cohesive discussion and/or argument based on what was witnessed. This treatise is meant to provide a lens, context, and support for research on African and African diaspora dance. Think of it as a concise paradigm handbook of sorts. Toward that end, the intent is to make the content in this book as accessible as possible to all. Accordingly, the terminology utilized in this work is meant to be clear, basic, and uncluttered by jargon. As researchers increase their studies on African dance and African body movements, they will learn to identify movements that are not included in this work as characteristically African, and they will develop the capacity to effectively include them in their arguments. This work is meant to establish a starting point – a long overdue universal frame of reference for organizing research on African and African diaspora dance.

Note

1 My first book, *History Dances: Chronicling the History of Traditional Mandinka Dance*, focuses on utilizing African dance systems as primary, African derived sources for constructing historical narratives about Africa. African dance systems include the dance itself, and all the elements that facilitate conveyance of the message that the dance is attempting to communicate. For a detailed definition of dance systems, see Ofosuwa Abiola, *History Dances: Chronicling the History of Traditional Mandinka Dance* (London: Routledge, 2019), 1–2.

1 Performative practices and documentation through an African lens

An introduction

Afrikinesis is a research paradigm and a methodology for research on African dance and African-oriented dance styles.[1] Research paradigms are philosophical frameworks that research is based on. They offer patterns of understanding from which the theories and practices of a research project can operate. The appropriate research paradigm can provide researchers with a wider lens, broader perspective, and a transparent, unfettered process for analysis in under-researched topics such as African and African diaspora dance styles. In addition, a research paradigm well suited for a particular research subject can simultaneously be utilized as a methodology. Fittingly, as a research paradigm, Afrikinesis provides a logical and intentional structure for conducting research on African and African diaspora dance, while facilitating deeper understanding and refining the quality of the research, transparency, and its proficiency.

The application of Afrikinesis in research also facilitates the identification and accurate categorization of dances, dance styles, movement vocabulary, and any phenomena related to dance that is founded on, emulates, imitates, or mirrors dances and body movements of African origin. It provides a roadmap for identifying the origin of contemporary and historic dances as a whole or African elements within such dances. Afrikinesis also serves as a template, format, and a strategic design for framing and situating research on African and African diaspora dance. With the number of paradigms currently at the disposal of researchers, one may ask, is there a need for another paradigm and why are existing paradigms inadequate? Thus, these questions must be addressed before all other discussions.

The need for a paradigm for research on African dance

It is not possible to place a number on phenomena worthy of research. As such topics are countless, they are also infinitely diverse. Alas, the fact remains that all research-worthy topics do not receive the same amount of attention from researchers, but they deserve such, and they also deserve the type of rigorous inquiry and the efficient organizational structure afforded by research paradigms. Fields well established in Western schools of thought often have several paradigms to facilitate the research process.[2] Under-researched subjects, such as African dance, possess few, if any, paradigms. African and African diaspora dance techniques including Kariamu Welsh's Umfundalai, the Katherine Dunham technique, and Germaine Acogny's modern African dance techniques to name a few do exist and are documented or at least acknowledged in the African and African diaspora dance community. However, paradigms for conducting research on such techniques or any other aspects of African and/or African diaspora dance are exceedingly scarce. More importantly, those few African dance research paradigms that do exist in the African dance community are largely undocumented.

Research paradigms are generally understood through Western lenses. They fall under two overarching categories – positivism (quantitative) and interpretivism (qualitative) – and commonly belong to the social science and philosophy paradigm tool kits. Other fields, including the humanities, the sciences, the arts, among others, utilize these frameworks as well, and other paradigms have sprung from these two foundational paradigm philosophies over the course of time. Positivism approaches the study of a topic from an empirical scientific methodology. It utilizes devices such as numbers, statistics, and controlled experiments. According to the positivism approach, studies should not extend beyond what can be observed. Interpretivism, on the other hand, assumes that all that comprises reality is subjective and constructed socially. Thus, interpretivism posits that reality is understood through the diverse experiences and histories of individuals, and it therefore differs for each individual. These Western understandings of research methods and paradigms are inadequate for research on African dance, because African dance systems do not fall neatly into either of these categories solely. As will be discussed later, for a dance to be identified as, derived from, or to contain elements of an African dance system, the dance must satisfy two criteria: the dance must contain one or more of the elements in the characteristically African body movement category, and one or more items in the African aesthetic group.

Characteristically African body movements are explicitly defined and can be empirically identified in dance by researchers (see Chapter 3). Whether the researchers are dance practitioners or not is a nonfactor for this observation. The body movements are observable and quantifiable. For example, a sample of 50 dances can be observed to identify the number of body movements that are characteristically African. For more specificity, the sample can be taken from a distinct location or from a specific ethnic group. With regard to interpretivism, one of the criteria for a dance to contain an African aesthetic is that the dance should exhibit the lived experiences of the people of the society it hails from. An example would be a traditional African dance that is a rain dance performed to avert a current or future drought similar to one that the people in the community experienced in the past.

As is clear in the aforementioned examples, to qualify as a dance that can be identified as, derived from, or contain elements of an African dance system, the dance must satisfy criteria from two areas – characteristically African body movements – and exhibit an African aesthetic. Accordingly, a framework for research on African dance should be able to employ both positivism and interpretivism methodologies as one paradigm. Proponents of Western research paradigms will argue that research on African dance can be conducted utilizing both systems. However, a paradigm best suited for research on African dance and African diaspora dance should hail from the worldview of people of African descent. Such a paradigm would meticulously address all necessary aspects of the study with a single system or methodology. Dances in Africa and in the African diaspora are vital components of a culture that reflects the lived experiences of the people that established the culture. African society is driven by its culture. Thus, adequate interpretation and comprehension of research on African and African-derived dances must be buttressed upon a system of understanding such research through an African cultural lens not a Western one.

The inadequacy of non-African-oriented research paradigms

As African and African diaspora dances and dance styles have their origin in the past with periods ranging from ancient eras to the recent past, it makes sense that the field of history is the foundational field for research on such dances. The field of history was founded upon the interrogation of written documents from the past. Thus, the written record is the primary source for constructing narratives of historic accounts. As such, some researchers have turned to an oral history paradigm to alleviate gaps in knowledge where a written record is either nonexistent or scarce. For oral history, human memory is the source for the paradigm. Memory as a source for a people's history is a paradigm that emerged in the period following the conclusion of World War II.[3] Although this "breakthrough" acknowledgment for the use of this alternative paradigm in the field of history was significant, an oral history framework or methodology is only partially useful for research on African dance. Since the histories of African dances are embodied, researchers are not restricted to rely on the sometimes precarious and/or incomplete memories of interviewees alone. What may not be remembered by the conscious mind is depicted in the dance, the step, the body movement, and so on. Thus, through the utilization of Afrikinesis as a paradigm, researchers will gain access to memories on the subconscious level as well as the conscious mind. As such, for memory interpretation, there is embodied reinforcement of the event or experience housed in the dance, body movement, or the step. Moreover, a compendium of events and experiences stored in the collective memory of a people as a group are also continually displayed throughout generations in the dances passed down through the ages.

Hermeneutic phenomenology has been widely used by researchers to understand lived experiences. The hermeneutic phenomenology method follows the interpretivism view that experiences can be interpreted and utilized as a base for information. This is a general Western model, and the unique experiences of people of African descent were not taken into account when it was devised. Interpretation of results from the utilization of this paradigm and the parent paradigm of phenomenology is through a Western lens and will therefore lack significant events and experiences of African and African diaspora people. The enslavement and colonization of people of African descent in Africa and the African diaspora provide a pantheon of experiences that Western researchers would only have access to through research frameworks and inquires, such as Afrikinesis, that engage Black people – the people that experienced the phenomena under study. Afrikinesis not only engages the people whose lived experiences are under study, but it also provides the conventions for interpreting and understanding such research through an African lens. The research paradigms devised by the West were not conceived with the experiences and culture of people of African descent in mind. Western research methodologies were built upon the foundation of Western experiences and Western culture. As a result, Western qualitative research paradigms and methodologies inevitably (whether intentional or not) approach and interpret research and its findings from the lens of the West or non-African at best, and colonizer or enslaver at worst. Although there have been people of non-African descent who have historically supported and fought alongside Africans and African diasporans in their quest for equity, research on African dance and culture will be most illuminating and transparent if a paradigm that is indigenous to the culture of people of African descent and the experiences of people of African descent as living components of that culture is employed.

An example of how Western perceptions in Western research frameworks can derail interpretations of research on African dance and culture is evident in Doris Guillen's article, "Qualitative Research: Hermeneutical Phenomenological Method."[4] It is noteworthy that, in the initial summary of the article, Guillen posits "This method constitutes rigorous and consisted processes of the ethical dimensions of the daily experience."[5] The term that is the elephant in the room in this quote is "ethical." The meaning of "ethical" is generally understood as: moral, virtuous, principled, and so on. The use of the word "ethical" denotes that a judgment or opinion with regard to morality or virtue is to be formed and applied to the dimensions of the daily experiences that are studied. Since the researcher in this regard does not embody the experiences to form opinions bathed in African or African diaspora experience, ethics in this paradigm are based on Eurocentric experiences and, by extension, Eurocentric standards of morality. The Afrikinesis paradigm specifically engages embodied African experiences and assesses those experiences through an African cultural lens, and thus discussions on morality or ethics will be founded on African worldviews. Consequently, the findings of research conducted via Eurocentric frameworks have historically been laden with ethnocentric and hegemonic narratives of African and African diaspora culture.

A word on ethnocentric and Eurocentric representations of African and African diaspora culture

Ethnocentrism is defined as the belief that one's own culture, ethnic group, nationality, and so on are superior to all others, and judges the value of others' cultural practices based on the standards of one's own. A historic example of ethnocentrism at work is evident in the chronicles written by Arab travelers to Africa during the precolonial period. The fourteenth-century Muslim chronicler, Ibn Battuta, employs ethnocentric bias in the documentation of his travels through medieval Mali. Islamic practice of the day frowned upon folk dance in general and African folk and traditional dance in particular. Ibn Battuta judged what he saw in Africa through an Islamic lens, where Islam and its tenets were held as superior to all others, and as the barometer through which other cultural practices were to be judged. In his description of a Mandinka griot performance, Ibn Battuta states:

> Each one of them [the griots] has got inside a costume made of feathers to look like a thrush with a wooden head made for it and a red beak as if it were the head of a bird. They stand before the sultan in that ridiculous attire and recite their poetry. . . . I was informed that this performance is old amongst them; they continued it from before Islam.[6]

Ibn Battuta's statement unwittingly reveals much about the incorporation of Mandinka philosophical tenets in griot performance during the medieval period and the age of such practice. Mandinka griots (known as jeli or jali depending on the region in Africa), from periods in the remote past to the present, were responsible for preserving the history of royal lineages, family lines, villages, and in some cases regions.[7] They memorized large quantities of information and conveyed such through music, dance, and poetic recitations. West African griots are currently witnessed singing histories while playing instruments such as balafons or koras and incorporating dance in the performance. Although modern-day griots' performance attire consists of some of the finest traditional African garments, they do not employ the masquerade element with the bird costume. Consequently, Ibn Battuta's passage unknowingly does reveal a past griot practice of incorporating Mandinka philosophy in griot performance but simultaneously omits the dance-posturing body movements that accompanied the recitations.[8] To fully comprehend the detrimental effects of his ethnocentric chronicles, basic knowledge of Mandinka philosophy must be discussed.

Birds in Mandinka philosophical systems represent a higher mind. They are perceived as a liaison between the heavens and the earth. When humans endeavor to communicate with the supreme creator, they must communicate through birds. Thus, the griots remembered and conveyed profuse amounts of information through dance, music, and song, and were therefore understood as the personification of a bird, or higher mind, communicating with higher realms – the heavens. Ibn Battuta's account also provided clues about the age of this practice when he stated, "it existed before Islam." Islam emerged in the Middle East in the seventh century and was introduced to Africa through various methods and through diverse periods. The Mandinka of medieval Mali was introduced to Islam in roughly the twelfth century. It can therefore be surmised that the practice of griots performing as bird masqueraders existed for at least 200 years before Ibn Battuta's fourteenth-century visit to the region since the practice existed "before Islam."[9] Ibn Battuta's ethnocentric assertion that the griot's traditional attire for such a performance is "ridiculous" devalues and dismisses the significance of the entire performance and its cultural history. Ibn Battuta's negative comments about this significant practice discourage efforts toward a more profound inquiry into the nature, purpose, and impact of these performances. Alas, the dance portion of the performance is completely omitted in his passage and the meaning and specific body movements employed are consequently lost.

The aforementioned example of Ibn Battuta's writing about African culture depicted through an ethnocentric lens is in and of itself enough to effectively illustrate why such an approach to African dance research and African culture generally can be culturally and historically damaging. However, there are also instances where researchers appear to be inclusive in their presentation of dance research but still approach the subject from a Eurocentric lens. Eurocentricity regards European culture as preeminent and often excludes other cultures. If non-European cultures are addressed, their significance is diminished. For example, in the book *American Dance: The Complete Illustrated History*, Margaret Fuhrer describes American tap dance as a combination of Irish tap and African-American tap dance styles.[10] African-American expressions of tap dance are discussed within an Irish-African-American perspective. According to Fuhrer, "After the Stono Insurrection laws prohibited black slaves from using drums in the mid-eighteenth century, they transferred their intricate West African drumming rhythms to their bodies, especially their feet."[11] She further discusses that the Slave Code of 1740 was enacted to prevent enslaved African Americans from drumming and dancing.[12] Therefore, Fuhrer essentially states that African Americans began to move their banned drum rhythms to their "bodies and their feet" in the mid-eighteenth century (i.e., the year 1740), which is a full century before the migration of multitudes of Irish immigrants to America in 1847.[13] The origin and expansion of

African-American tap dance 100 years before the large-scale migration of the Irish to the United States are not discussed. The Stono Insurrection in 1739, which resulted in drum banning legislation in 1740 and increased utilization of percussive dances and percussive body movements among the African-American dance community, is mentioned, but the evolution of such movements into dance styles such as tap and juba (later known as step-dancing) over the 100-year period prior to the large-scale introduction of Irish dance is not expounded on. Moreover, Fuhrer makes the contradictory statement that the formation of African-American tap dance styles occurred at the same time the Irish entered the United States in the mid-nineteenth century (i.e., the 1840s) and that African Americans adapted the Irish tap dance movements into their dances. This Eurocentric view not only wipes out an entire century of African-American dance evolution, innovation, narratives, and so on, but it also discredits significant African-American dance contributions to Irish tap dance in the United States as well. Once the Irish settled into the American cultural landscaping, many Irish entertainers became participants in minstrelsy in the late 1840s and 1850s. Minstrelsy, as nefarious and culturally damaging as it was, nonetheless was founded on – albeit, by making fun of – African-American dance and body movements. The Minstrelsy practitioners would perform their rendition of African-American dance and incorporate a few Irish dance steps. Although minstrelsy received a wide amount of attention in the book *American Dance*, the fact that, within that genre of dance, the Irish incorporated African-American dance movements into their routines is briefly mentioned, but not expounded upon.

African-American tap dance is founded on African dances that were retained on plantations and passed down through the generations. Thus, the narratives, lived experiences, and significance of the movements that ultimately comprised African-American tap dance were unaddressed in Fuhrer's *American Dance*. Dance research presented through Eurocentric lenses often omits significant African and African diaspora experiences, history, and culture. Subsequently, to avert the occurrence of cultural and historical misrepresentation at best, and total omission at worst, African and African diaspora dance research should be grounded within an Afrikinesis methodology and paradigm. As a result, the documentation of such will reflect the contributions, innovations, and evolution of African dance with regard to the overall field of dance studies.

Appropriation, the larger picture

Appropriation is the act of utilizing or performing another's works, productions, art, culture, and so on, presenting it as one's own, and not obtaining permission from the true creators, and/or not giving credit to the actual progenitors as the creators of the work. When dance and other cultural systems are not documented, they can become "orphaned culture" where no person or group is recognized for creating it. Instances of orphaned culture include, but are not limited to, American jazz dance, American tap, American hip hop, and so on. When culture is orphaned, it not only opens the door for cultural appropriation, but it facilitates it. The word "American" in these examples refers to the country not an ethnic group. Since designations such as American jazz dance do not indicate any particular ethnic group as the originator, anyone can claim to be its creator. What is worst, when culture is orphaned, it is not perceived to be the innovation of any one group, and therefore, all Americans regardless of their ethnicity can claim jazz dance as their invention. Jazz dance is the result of African Americans' practice of retaining and incorporating African dance movements with new dance styles that result from their experiences in America. African Americans are the progenitors of jazz dance, but the designation American jazz dance does not recognize their cultural invention, nor does it acknowledge the significance of their cultural contribution. Thus, with regard to orphaned culture, the act of appropriation with impunity becomes an effortless act to accomplish and it becomes impossible to hold a single perpetrator accountable for the appropriated activity. Accordingly, to prevent the prevalence of orphaning culture originated by people of African descent and to avert appropriation of African descents' cultural phenomena, the cultural phenomena must be documented. The vital undertaking of documenting culture is not generally practiced by people of African descent worldwide. Yet it is imperative that dances, dance styles, body movements, movement vocabulary, dance history, dance theories, dance research frameworks, dance systems, and everything in between and beyond that are of African origin are documented. As such, the purpose of this book is:

- To contribute to the crucial, scarcely endeavored work of documenting African dance research paradigms and methodologies.
- To provide a structure that is specifically suited for research on African and African diaspora dance that can be utilized by researchers who are nondancers, researchers who are dancers, dance historians, critics, and theorists in and beyond the field of dance studies.
- Provide a way forward for addressing and preventing appropriation of African and African diaspora dance and dance culture.

Toward this end, Chapter 1 will introduce the Afrikinesis paradigm and emphasize its importance for research on African and African diaspora dance. The introduction is the preliminary chapter that defines paradigms in general and discusses the need for a research paradigm uniquely positioned to address African and African diaspora dance. Western paradigms are also mentioned to illustrate their inadequacy with regard to research on African and African diaspora dance systems. Examples are discussed to provide evidence for the argument that researchers of African cultural systems generally, and African dance systems specifically, should utilize a paradigm that hails from the worldview and/or culture of people of African descent. The introduction concludes with a synopsis for each of the chapters that follow.

Chapter 2 discusses the overarching universal tenets of culture in Africa. The unique nature of African culture and its capacity to be reflected in all aspects of its branches are delineated. This chapter also articulates the importance of differentiating between a trend and authentic culture by examining the elements that comprise culture. In this chapter, there is also a discussion of, and a definition of, the African aesthetic in dance, and this chapter underscores the cultural signs that facilitate the recognition and proper identification of the African aesthetic. This chapter then highlights the importance of the African aesthetic with regard to the Afrikinesis paradigm. Finally, Chapter 2 defines the African dance system and delineates its importance for understanding research on African dance.

Chapter 3 delineates the diverse pantheon of distinct body movements that comprise African dance. To gain a comprehensive understanding, this chapter discusses the parts of the body, and how their combination of movements comprises African dance. Recognizing African dance movements when witnessed is crucial for appropriately applying the Afrikinesis paradigm to African dance research. As such, Chapter 3 portrays the diverse pantheon of distinct body movements that comprise African dance. To gain a comprehensive understanding, this chapter discusses the parts of the body, and how their combination of movements comprises African dance. Terminology for engaging African dance systems is disclosed as well as cautionary hints for identifying movements that are sometimes missed by the untrained eye.

Chapter 4 introduces the researcher to the research principles required to apply an Afrikinesis framework to their study. It is not enough to understand that a paradigm specifically suited for a particular type of research is paramount, effective application of that paradigm is also critical. As such, specific terms are defined and delineated, and the process for situating a research project or topic within an Afrikinesis paradigm is meticulously discussed. Finally, case studies that demonstrate how the Afrikinesis paradigm can be applied to research on African and African diaspora dance are discussed.

Finally, Chapter 5 concludes the conversation by synthesizing the discussions and evidence into a conceptual organic whole and a call to action for researchers. The conclusion recounts the significance of understanding the universal tenets of African culture, while placing equal importance on the distinctions of the diverse ethnicities in Africa when conducting African dance research. It also accentuates the fact that, after obtaining the tools afforded by application of the Afrikinesis paradigm, the researcher can present a substantiated and compelling argument in support of their distinct topic within the African and African diaspora dance pantheon.

Notes

1. The term "Afrikinesis" is a compilation of two words, "Afri" from the word African and "kinesis" which is defined as body movement. I coined this designation for this paradigm because it describes the most basic element in a dance, the movement of the body, and it identifies the people and the location of focus. Hence, the word itself provides clues regarding the nature and appropriate application – that is, research on African and African-oriented dances and body movements – for the paradigm and methodology.
2. Western schools of thought in this study include Europe and the United States.
3. See Alister Thompson, "Four Paradigm Transformations in Oral History," *The Oral History Review* 34, no. 1 (Winter-Spring 2007): 49.
4. See Doris Elida and Fuster Guillen, "Qualitative Research: Hermeneutical Phenomenological Method," *Propósitos y Representaciones* 7, no. 1 (January-April 2019), https://files.eric.ed.gov/fulltext/EJ1212514.pdf.
5. See Elida and Guillen, "Qualitative Research," 217.
6. See Said Hamdun and Noël King, *Ibn Battuta in Black Africa* (Princeton: Markus Wiener Publishers, 2010), 53–54. A griot is an oral historian-musician who conveys history through song, dance, chants, and poems.
7. In Mandinka culture, a griot is called a jeli or jali. The difference in spelling denotes regional differences in pronunciation. The French spelling, djeli/djali, is also widely used.
8. Patrick R. McNaughton, *A Bird Dance Near Saturday City: Sidi Ballo and the Art of West African Masquerade* (Bloomington: Indiana University Press, 2008), 234.
9. In this example, I will use the introduction of Islam to medieval Mali in twelfth century as a frame of reference for the phrase "before Islam." However, the practice of the griot bird masquerader could be older if Ibn Battuta was referring to the advent of Islam in the Middle East in the seventh century.
10. See Margaret Fuhrer, *American Dance: The Complete Illustrated History* (Minneapolis: Voyageur Press, 2014).
11. Ibid., 53. The Stono Insurrection (also known as the Stono Rebellion) is a slave revolt that occurred in 1739 in South Carolina. The enslaved Africans marched through the streets drumming, shouting liberty, and inviting more slaves to join their cause. Roughly 100 slaves had joined before the insurrection was halted by a large band of armed white slave owners. Since slave owners witnessed that drums used for dance could also be used for revolt, by 1740, legislation was enacted in South Carolina that included a ban on drumming in the Slave Code of the state. The ban on drumming then spread to other states.
12. See Fuhrer, *American Dance*, 33.
13. A disease that affected Ireland's primary staple crop created a famine that killed more than one million people from 1847 to 1851. This event was called "The Potato Famine" or "The Irish Famine." To seek refuge, up to two million Irish set sails for the United States beginning in 1847 and continued until 1851. The potato crops in Ireland did not fully recover until 1852.

2 Overview of African culture and its reflection on dance

African culture

African culture is a visible and cohesive compilation of numerous phenomena. It is a reflection of all that is universally African on a wholistic level, while simultaneously divulging a diverse macrocosm of distinct customs, environments, climates, sensibilities, and ethnicities. African culture is a smorgasbord of lived experiences, wherein continental commonalities and distinct practices garner equal value. African culture includes dance and the arts, language, the educational system, religion, philosophy, mythology, literature (oral and written), identity (individual and group), and all that African societies are built upon. It is not enough to be a passing trend, regardless of how significant that trend may appear in the present, to qualify as culture, it must be retained – passed down through the generations (familial and/or community). As such, African culture has been passed down through the generations on and beyond the African continent by African descendants living throughout the world. African culture can be recent, that is, two or three generations old and counting, ancient, or it could have fallen out of practice (obsolete). As such, African cultural tenets specifically, and cultural elements in general, can also be born, renewed, and can die. African culture is functional, practical, and at the same time artistic and beautiful. In Africa, culture drives the society, and dance is an essential component of African culture.

Religious systems are a crucial element within African culture, and dance plays a central role in all African religious systems. Religious systems inform thought, the way the world is interacted with, and the way the world is perceived. As posited by John Mbiti:

> African religion is the product of the thinking and experiences of our forefathers and mothers, that is men, women and children of former generations. They formed religious ideas, they formulated religious beliefs, they observed religious ceremonies and rituals, they told proverbs and myths which carried religious meanings, and they evolved laws and customs which safeguarded the life of the individual and his community.[1]

DOI: 10.4324/9781003462491-2

According to Kongo cosmology, in the beginning, there was a world without visible life. Although there was an emptiness of visible phenomena, it was filled with invisible activity.[2] As a result, people's lives are surrounded by diverse invisible forces and vibrations that govern the lives of human beings. Accordingly, spiritual systems in Africa include an instructional pathway for harmonious interactions between people and the invisible forces that populate their world. A common thread of understanding traverses through all religions in Africa. Thus, the plural term "religious systems" should be understood in the sense that each ethnic group, society, and so on has the same religious understandings, aspirations, and goals, but they achieve such through various distinct methods. Nonetheless, it is understood that the commonalities far outnumber and outweigh the differences. Moreover, the rite of passage process in Africa (see Chapter 4) has historically been a requirement for all members of the society. The rite of passage process equipped everyone – kings, farmers, noblemen, artisans, and so on – with the same profound ancient knowledge of the ages, as equals. Historically, in Africa, there was no separation of church and state. People's navigation through society was expected to be via a system of connections with the visible – nature, people, institutions, and so on – and the invisible – ancestors, deities, energies, vibrations, and so on.

The manners in which the society functions are derived from the culture of that society, religion is a crucial part of African culture, and dance is a vital part of African religion. As African culture exhibits an aesthetic specific to it, so too does African dance, the child of African culture, exhibit an aesthetic specific to it. In addition to understanding African culture, knowledge of African dance aesthetics is crucial for understanding and for the appropriate application of the Afrikinesis paradigm for research on African dance.

The African dance aesthetic

Although the African aesthetic is grossly under-researched, there are scholars in the field who have contributed significant work on the subject. In Kwasi Wiredu's edited work, *A Companion to African Philosophy*, both Nkiru Nzegwu's chapter, "Art and Community: A Social Conception of Beauty and Individuality" and Ajume H. Wingo's chapter, "The Many-Layered Aesthetics of African Art," make phenomenal contributions to the understanding of aesthetics from an African perspective.[3] Equally important are Kariamu Welsh's edited work, *The African Aesthetic: Keeper of the Traditions*. Her chapter on the "Aesthetic Conceptualization of Nzuri" provides an enlightening presentation on the African aesthetic from an African diaspora lens.[4] Yvonne Daniel's *Dancing Wisdom: Embodied Knowledge in Haitian Vodou, Cuban Yoruba, and Bahian Candomblé* includes a thought-provoking discussion on the aesthetic system that buttresses African diaspora dance.[5] There are other conversations on African aesthetics, but there are not enough. To grasp a thorough understanding of the African dance aesthetic and all its complexities, there must be numerous and diverse discourses perceived and explained through different lenses on the subject. Hence, the African dance aesthetic, as understood and applied in the Afrikinesis paradigm, will be discussed in this study.

An African dance aesthetic must reflect the types of movement understood to be characteristically African.[6] The definition of an African dance aesthetic cannot mimic the commonly understood definition of aesthetic because that definition utilizes European value systems as a standard barometer. African dance body movements were created in Africa to appeal to an African constituency and according to African social norms, practices, rituals, worldview, and decorum. They speak to African societies. This fact does not preclude the ability of African dances and arts to appeal to people that originate outside of the African continent, but African value systems must be kept in mind as the standard barometer when attempting to identify and assess African-oriented dances. Particular attention should be paid when studying dances performed in a contemporary setting and to dances that are not generally thought of as African, but that blatantly contain African dance elements. With regard to African traditional arts, there is no such thing as art (in this case dance) created for the sake of art. Traditional dances specifically, and arts generally, in Africa are functional as well as beautiful.

To define the African dance aesthetic for the purpose of the Afrikinesis paradigm, at least three criteria must be observed:

1. The dance under study must include movements that are characteristically African and/or movements that are location-specific African movements.[7]
2. The dance, dance movement, dance system, or dance step should display current culture while simultaneously housing and displaying dance history.
3. There should be a relationship between the dance system and the lived experiences of the people in the community.

Unpacking African dance aesthetics

The first criterion in the definition of the African dance aesthetic is that the dance under study must include movements that are characteristically African and/or movements that are location-specific African movements. This criterion requires a firm knowledge of the process of identifying African body movements. The method for identifying African dance body movements and their unique descriptions is discussed in detail in Chapter 3. To summarize, each movement performed by the body has significance. It either tells a story in and of itself or is part of a step, dance, or dance system that conveys a larger narrative. The ability to identify the movement's origin – African, European, and so on – greatly increases the researcher's ability to comprehend and communicate the narratives that a dance is conveying.

The second criterion is that the dance, dance movement, dance system, or dance step should display current culture while simultaneously housing and displaying dance history. To address this criterion, the researcher must ask questions including but not limited to:

- Although the dance may be historic or traditional, have new movements been introduced to the dance that are noticeably more recent than the original steps and are performed alongside or curated along with the original steps or body movements?
- Are different or more current materials presently used for the attire or props when compared with the original materials that have been historically used?
- Is the dance presently performed in a different location than the original historic location?
- Has the gender of the dance practitioners changed or does the dance or dance narrative currently also include a gender that was historically omitted?

It is worth mentioning that if a traditional dance or body movement is executed during this current time period, it automatically qualifies the body movement for the first part of this criterion – displaying "current culture." Regardless of the antiquity of the dance or body movement, if it is executed today, it is a part of the current displays of culture.

Finally, for a dance to exhibit an African dance aesthetic under the guidelines of the Afrikinesis paradigm, there should be a relationship between the dance system and the lived experiences of the people in the community. A question to ask oneself when engaging this criterion is, does the dance system contain narratives of events or experiences that occurred in the community of the dance progenitors? An example of what to look for in an effort to address this question is a dance or specialized body movements exclusively performed at funerals, religious, or other ceremonies or events in the African or African diaspora community that the dance hails from. Another example of what to look for in an effort to address this criterion is a body movement that has been passed down through generations and is apparent in current dances regardless of the genre of dance, such as a pelvic contraction (see Chapter 3 later for a definition of pelvic contraction). In other words, body movements that are continually passed on to subsequent generations have significance in the community of people retaining the movement. It is the researcher's job to learn what that significance is and all that it implies.

The aforementioned questions are not exhaustive, but they provide a starting point for unearthing the type of rich narratives that can be ascertained from a research framework and methodology designed specifically for a distinct type of research. To fully understand the criteria described earlier, the definitions of dance systems, cultural diffusion, syncretism, and the African diaspora are discussed later. Fuller comprehension will require additional definitions discussed in Chapter 3, including characteristically African body movements, parts of the body, dance steps, torso positions, among others.

The dance system

Traditional African dance must be studied as a system. Since traditional African dances house historic and cultural information, to effectively engage the dance narrative, all of the elements necessary for the performance of the African dance must be considered as part and parcel of the dance (see *Table* A in the Appendix). As such, in addition to the physical execution of the dance itself, the attire the dancers are wearing, the musicians and their attire, the location where the dance is performed, the time of year, the instruments the musicians are playing, the props used by the dancers and drummers, the color scheme of the attire, the spectators (or lack thereof) and the songs sung (or not sung) must be studied as integral parts of the dance – hence the term "dance system."

Cultural diffusion versus syncretism

Researchers of African dance history must be cognizant of instances where cultural diffusion and where syncretism has occurred within the continent of Africa. Cultural diffusion with regard to African dance systems or African body movements exists when elements of the dance system or when body movements from one culture or ethnic group are spread to and executed by another. For example, the djembe drums are part of a West African ethnic group's dance system.[8] The ethnic group is the Mandinka, and the drums are constructed to be played while the drummer is standing with the drum hanging between both legs. The drum has a large head surface where the skin is attached contrasted with a narrow trunk with no skin on the bottom. Ropes are wrapped and tied to the drum in the fashion of a backpack, to facilitate the drum to hang just below the waist while being played. The ngoma drum, a part of the dance systems witnessed in the Democratic Republic of the Congo and the surrounding areas of Central Africa, is constructed to be played while it stands on its own "feet." The drum is tall to prevent the musician from having to bend over to play it. The ngoma drum has a round head surface and the trunk gradually tapers from the middle to the bottom, but without the large contrast that is witnessed between the head and trunk in the West African Mandinka djembe drum. The bottom of the ngoma drum has feet to facilitate stabilization and its foundation on the ground while the drummer plays it. The traditional ngoma drum was obviously constructed to stand on its own while being played. However, recently, I witnessed a traditional Congolese dance troupe performing traditional or folk dances in traditional Congolese attire. The drummers had tied ropes to their ngoma drums in the same fashion as those tied to the djembe drums of Mandinka dance systems in West Africa and they played their Congolese rhythms with the ngoma drums hanging from just below their waists. Thus, cultural diffusion was present between dance systems of West and Central Africa.

Syncretism exists when separate dance system elements or body movements from different ethnic groups, cultures, or areas of the world are combined to create a new dance or dance system. Syncretism is witnessed exceedingly in the African diaspora, where African cultural elements are fused with Western elements and in some cases Indian or indigenous elements. For example, in Central America and the Caribbean, the Garifuna's traditional dance systems include elements of African, Arawak, and Carib Indian culture.[9] Additionally, the Garifuna's traditional style of dress displays apparent influences of African, Indian and European styles. Their language is a syncretization of African languages and the Arawak language. Another example of syncretism is witnessed in the Yoruba religious ceremonial dances practiced in Brazil. The Yoruba religion in Brazil is called Candomblé. The ceremonies, religious tenets, drumming, dancing are unquestionably African. However, the attire worn during the religious ceremonies displays Portuguese influences. The traditional African songs are sung in Portuguese and so on. Hence, the influences from the different cultures are merged to form a unique culture, while retaining its African core.

Why the African diaspora is significant

In recognition of the plights – historic and current – of the 200 million people of African descent in the Americas and the millions more in other parts of the world, the United Nations has declared the years 2015–2024 the International Decade for People of African Descent.[10] The magnitude of the aforementioned declaration cannot be overstated. What is significant is the overwhelmingly huge number – literally hundreds of millions – of people of African descent living outside of the continent of Africa, and the number is increasing. Hence, the culture, worldview, and extended history of the African continent must, if for no other reason than the sheer numbers of African diaspora people, have a significant cultural impact on the world. As such, African cultural tenets generally and African derived dances specifically are performed and witnessed throughout the world.

Notes

1 John S. Mbiti, *Introduction to African Religion*, 2nd ed. (Long Grove: Waveland Press Inc., 1991), 14.
2 See Kimbwandende K.B. Fu-Kiau, *African Cosmology of the Bantu-Kongo: Principles of Life and Living* (Middletown: African Tree Press, 2001), 17–18.
3 See Kwasi Wiredu, *A Companion to African Philosophy*, ed. Nkiru Nzegwu and Ajume H. Wingo (Malden: Blackwell Publishing Ltd., 2004), 415–24 and 425–32.
4 See Kariamu Welsh-Asante, ed., *The African Aesthetic: Keeper of the Traditions* (Westport: Praeger, 1993), 1–18.
5 See Yvonne Daniel, *Dancing Wisdom: Embodied Knowledge in Haitian Vodou, Cuban Yoruba, and Bahian Candomblé* (Urbana: University of Illinois Press, 2005).

Overview of African culture and its reflection on dance 17

6 For a discussion on characteristically African body movements, see Chapter 3.
7 Location-specific African dance movements are discussed in Chapter 3 in this work.
8 Djembe drums are a part of Mandinka dance systems. "Djembe" is the French spelling, but when pronounced in English, the letter "d" is silent.
9 The Garifuna are an Afro-Caribbean people who were enslaved West Africans that escaped captivity and washed up on the shores of the Caribbean Island of St. Vincent in roughly 1635. They intermarried with the Arawak and the Carib Indians. Presently, there are approximately 300,000 Garifunas worldwide, with a notable number living in the United States and Canada. Garifuna communities along the Caribbean Sea live primarily in towns along the coasts and villages in the Central American countries of Guatemala, Belize, Nicaragua and Honduras. See Joseph O. Palacio, ed., *The Garifuna: A Nation Across Borders, Essays in Social Anthropology* (Benque Viejo del Carmen, Belize: Cubola Books, 2005).
10 See the United Nations website, https://www.un.org/en/observances/decade-people-african-descent for the proclamation and program of activities regarding the International Decade for People of African Descent.

3 Identifying African dance body movements

In African dance, each movement performed by the body has significance. It either tells a story in and of itself or is part of a step, dance, or dance system that conveys a larger narrative. The body has the capacity to bend, jump, sway, glide, kick, shuffle, squat, and so on in countless ways. The utilization of any research paradigm necessitates a common frame of reference. For a broad spectrum of researchers to make the most efficient use of a paradigm, the paradigm should be free of incomprehensible jargon and/or over complex terminology. Straightforward language should be used and definitions of such be disclosed early in the discussion. To that end, the parts of the body and the parts of a dance warrant attention in this study.

Body movement versus dance step

For the purposes of this framework, a body movement is defined as the most rudimentary movements of the body – for example, the singular movement of the head in a forward direction or lifting the right leg at any height. A dance step is comprised of two or more body movements together or in a sequence or pattern. For instance, the movement of the head forward while lifting the right leg would be considered a step. To execute a dance step, the body movements need not be executed at the same pace or at the same time. The building blocks of a choreographic work are the steps which are comprised of a parade of body movements.

Root step

The root step is the original dance step or original series of body movements, devised before all others in a particular dance. The root steps are the foundational steps and contain the most historic information than any other steps. Root steps can be basic, complex, in-between, or a combination of both basic and complex. The root step does not change over time and is passed down through the generations. Root steps are consciously and, in many cases, unconsciously transferred to posterity. The vast majority of African-based body movements witnessed in the African diaspora today are root steps – many of which were retained and transferred to current generations instinctively.

In addition to root steps, other types of body movements that fall under the category of steps include basic and complex steps. Basic steps are comprised of simple body movements and usually only display three of four body movements. The body movements in basic steps are easily identifiable. For example, a basic step may be executed by lifting the right leg, bobbing the head forward, and waving the left arm. The body movements may or may not be executed simultaneously. Complex steps require a multitude of body movements, some may be executed simultaneously, others in succession. Complex steps may include pauses, false steps (defined later), subtle movements, and body movements executed at different rhythms and times.

Auxiliary movements

Auxiliary body movements are body movements that are added to root steps and to the movement vocabulary (discussed later) for narrative emphasis and for creativity. Auxiliary body movements contribute to the overall message that a dance conveys. Such creative and often flamboyant body movements can disguise steps. Thus, it is important to scrutinize steps meticulously to separate the aspects of the step that can be categorized as the root from the parts of the step that are more akin to the "dressing."

The dance

A dance is comprised of a series of curated steps woven together to tell a story. The building blocks to dances are steps, and the foundational elements of steps are body movements. All traditional African dances, and by extension, African-oriented dances retained in the African diaspora, have meaning, and therefore all such dances tell stories. Additionally, all traditional African dances contain at least one root step. As a result, the stories the dances tell may or may not be in the conscious minds of the dancers performing or choreographers curating the dances, but they nonetheless house stories from their African root.

In Chart 3.1, illustrations 1, 3, and 4 depict torsos in the various acute positions executed during African and African-oriented dances and body movements. Illustration 2 depicts the position the torso exhibits when it is not in an acute position. Although acute torsos are categorized as characteristically African, dances and body movements do not need to contain acute torso positions to be of African origin.

20 *Identifying African dance body movements*

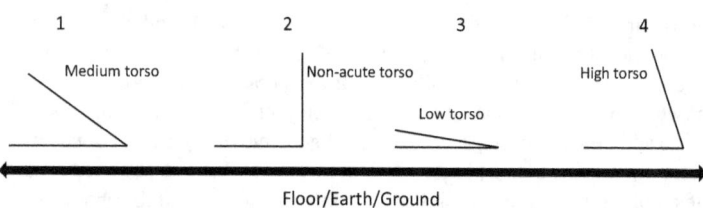

Chart 3.1 Torso Angles

The torso and torso positions

The torso is located in the upper region of the body between the armpits and the lower part of the waist. It is the region above the hips, and it houses the ribcage and subsequently the lungs. The chest, back, and both sides of the body are included. In many African dances, the torso is held over the feet and at a position that is less than 90° to the surface of the earth (or the ground). The term for such is "acute" (less than 90°). Acute torso positions can be executed at both extremes as long as they do not exceed or equal an angle of 90° to the surface of the earth.[1] They can be close to an angle of 90°; for example, a torso held at an angle of 88° to the surface of the earth would still be considered acute. Acute torso positions can also be witnessed at as little as ten degrees to the surface of the earth.

Acute torso positions can be executed with straight or bent knees, or while leaping or in low squats. Acute torso positions are high, medium, or low (see Chart 3.1 [torso angles]). Some high acute torso positions appear to be executed with a straight or vertical torso. Examining and comparing the angle of the dancer's back with regard to the level surface of the ground/earth will provide more clues regarding the torso position. If the torso appears to be close to parallel to the earth's surface, the torso is in a low acute torso position (see Figure 3.2 [low torso]). If the back of the dancer appears to be straight from the front of the dancer, but from the side there is a slight angle, then a high acute torso position is being witnessed (see Figure 3.3 [high torso]). The medium acute torso position is not only noticeably much lower than 90° to the surface of the earth, or noticeably not perpendicular to the earth, but also conspicuously much higher than a parallel position to the earth (see Figure 3.4 [medium torso]). It should be noted that a bow in a dance, such as those witnessed in European Ballroom dances such as Waltzes and similar dances, should not be misconstrued to be a dance movement executed with an acute torso. In African dances that include acute torsos, the entire movement is executed with the torso positioned over the feet at an angle (high, medium, or low) to the earth. Unlike dance movements completely executed with an acute angle, a dance movement that includes a bow requires for the torso to return to an erect position for proper execution of the dance movement.

Identifying African dance body movements 21

Figure 3.2 Low Torso

The photograph depicts the author executing a dance step that employs a low torso.
Photograph: Araku Abiola, 2006.

Torso contractions

A torso contraction is the frontward and backward movements of the torso. The frontward movement is executed by pushing the ribcage forward and simultaneously arching the back. The backward movement is executed by pushing the ribcage backward while simultaneously forming a concave shape

22 *Identifying African dance body movements*

Figure 3.3 High Torso

The photograph depicts a front shot of the author performing a dance step that employs a high acute torso. Photograph: Araku Abiola, 2005.

with the chest – in other words, the torso or chest contracts. Although the torso contraction only involves the movements and parts of the body described earlier, in actual dances, other parts of the body are sometimes incorporated to emphasize the torso contraction or to add additional lines and context to improvised and/or planned choreography. For example, placing the hands on

Figure 3.4 Medium Torso

The photograph depicts the author performing with her dance company, Suwabi African Ballet, executing a dance step that employs a medium torso.

Photograph: Araku Abiola, 2008.

the hips while performing a torso contraction will incorporate the shoulders and the forward and backward movement of the elbows in the torso contraction movement. However, the authentic, pure torso contraction does not include the shoulders, arms, and elbows.

A torso contraction for the purposes of this paradigm must include both the forward and backward movements of the chest executed as one body movement. Body movements that involve only the contraction of the torso or the creation of a concave shape with the chest without the forward motion as an equal part of the body movement are not considered a pure contraction. The opposite is also true. A body movement that involves the forward thrust of the chest, without an equal thrust backward is not considered a pure contraction for the purposes of this study on African and African diaspora dance and body movements. These incomplete torso contractions can be executed from two positions. The torso can be positioned or held in its natural place at the center, and from there, concave the chest; or from its natural position at the center, the torso can be pushed forward slightly to emphasize the backward contraction of the ribcage. Such incomplete contractions often involve a movement pause to create an emphasis in the lines the movement creates with the body. However, an authentic torso contraction involves the forward and backward movements of the torso where both movements are executed together as one step. Semi torso contractions or partial torso contractions still involve forward and backward movements of the torso, but the torso travels less distance to the front and/or back. Semi torso contractions can also be executed in double time, or much faster than complete contractions. Torso movements that involve right and left movements of the ribcage are not torso contractions. Similarly, circular movements of the chest or ribcage are not torso contractions.

Pelvic contractions

The pelvis or pelvic area of the body is located directly under the torso and under the waist. It includes the hips and end where the legs are connected to the hips.[2] Similar to the torso, the pelvic region includes the front, back, and both sides of the body in that region. A pelvic contraction involves the forward and backward movements of the pelvis. Unlike torso contractions which can be executed with straight or bent knees, pelvic contractions are executed primarily with bent knees to facilitate execution of the movement. Often, pelvic contractions are accompanied by torso contractions. However, when body movements are presented in this fashion, it should be understood that two separate movements (two separate contractions) are being witnessed.

Movements characteristically African

African dance movements that are referred to as characteristically African contain body movements that are not specific to any region or ethnicity and are witnessed throughout the continent of Africa.[3] These movements provide visual recognizable constructs of the African dance aesthetic. They do not require a trained eye or practitioner expertise to recognize them.

Identifying African dance body movements 25

Characteristically African dance movements include:

- Semi- or full contractions of the torso or pelvic region of the body, at fast or slow speeds. Contractions can be executed alone or in combination with each other or with other movements.
- Swift movements of the head, often circular but can be executed in a variety of directions.
- Hip movements from side to side and/or circular hip movements.
- Pelvic body movements from side to side and/or circular pelvic directions.
- Simultaneous diverse body movements, which employ parts of the body above and below the waist at different paces or cross-rhythms to each other.
- Body movements executed with the torso slanted over the feet at diagonal (acute) angles to the earth.
- Leaps of various heights performed with bent knees, parallel legs, and the torso held at an acute angle while in the air.
- Movements initiated from bent knees with legs parallel to each other.
- Polyrhythmic body movements (diverse body movements that exhibit two or more rhythmic patterns executed simultaneously).
- Syncopated body movements (accenting steps that would normally be subtle or recessive).

Location-specific African body movements

While characteristically African body movements can be witnessed throughout the continent of Africa, location-specific African body movements are witnessed more at distinct locations or among distinct ethnic groups in Africa. These movements are still undeniably African and are generally witnessed neither in the traditional and folk dances of Europe nor in other areas outside of the African continent, but they are executed more abundantly in specific locales in Africa than in others. Additionally, because a body movement is identified with a specific location in Africa, it does not preclude the possibility of its performance in an African location outside of the identified location of the movement. For example, torso contractions are witnessed more abundantly in traditional or historic dances practiced by various ethnic groups in West Africa, including but not limited to the polities of Mali, Nigeria, Gambia, Senegal, and Ghana, among others. Nonetheless, torso contractions can also be witnessed in the North-Central African country, Chad, while executing a dance called klag, and in the East African country, Ethiopia, while performing the eskista dance. Although many of the traditional or folk dances witnessed in Southern Africa do not generally employ torso contractions, it is still a possibility that the practitioners of some of these dances may.

26 Identifying African dance body movements

Alternatively, there are body movements that are witnessed exclusively in a specific location in Africa or performed specifically by a particular ethnic group. An example would be the high kick of the South African Zulu dances, indlamu, the males' warrior dance, and ingoma, the unisex social dance. Both of these Zulu dances include a body movement that involves kicking one leg so high that the foot points straight to the sky. This kick is executed with an acute torso, a flat foot, and the head bends down to meet the leg. Most African dance systems do not employ kicks as high as those witnessed in indlamu and ingoma. However, the execution of this kick is irrefutably African. The guidelines within the Afrikinesis paradigm will equip researchers with the ability to make a meticulous assessment of such body movements (see African Aesthetic later) and it will facilitate appropriate classification within the cornucopia of African dance movements regardless of where they are witnessed within or outside of the continent of Africa.

Dancing outside the box

There are complex African dance steps that contain body movements that fall outside of general movements usually witnessed within basic steps. Pauses are elements of certain complex steps that contain a halt or a sometimes barely discernable freeze in movement while executing the dance step. Subtle body movements also exist within certain African dance steps and are equally undiscernible if one does not apply meticulous attention to the movement under study.

Polyrhythmic body movements are performed by moving different parts of the body with two or more rhythmic patterns simultaneously. Polyrhythmic body movements usually employ several basic steps, that is, movements of the arms, or a hip movement, at different rhythms concurrently.

Syncopated body movements are also performed in traditional African dances and African diaspora dances. Syncopated body movements are witnessed when steps that would normally be subtle or recessive are accented and brought to a prominent position. These steps are usually executed in unexpected spaces in the dance.

False steps and false falls within a step are also exhibited in complex African dance steps. False steps are also known as a false foot movement. A false step is executed by appearing to place the foot on one area of the floor, and just before the foot touches the floor, the dancer unexpectedly places the foot somewhere else. False falls are executed when the dancer appears to trip over one of their feet and acts as though they are about to fall but gains composure at the last moment before they actually reach the ground.[4]

Natural body movements

African culture is communal. Its communal nature can be witnessed as a whole and through individual components of the culture. African dance is a component of the culture and therefore contains dances, and specific dance movements that are designed to be accessible to all in the community. The aspects of these dances that facilitate accessibility are the natural body movements. Natural body movements are movements that emulate stances and positions that the body naturally performs during daily tasks and through gestures performed subconsciously. Natural body movements include movements executed from bent knees, parallel legs and/or feet, acute torso, and so on. Such movements can be performed by people of diverse ages and abilities and do not require special dance training or schooling to perform. Harvest dances often contain natural body movements imitating planting gestures, the movements in religious dances emulate worshipping gestures, movements in ritualistic dances imitate the tasks to be performed for the ritual, and so on.

Dance considerations

To avert confusion, there should be a discussion on the distinctions between steps, body movements, and a dance. As discussed earlier, body movements are the basic movements and positioning of parts of the body such as lifting the head or raising a leg. Body movements are the building blocks of a step. A step is comprised of a combination of body movements to create a specific visual picture. The body movements are the building blocks for the step. There are body movements that are categorized as characteristically African. These movements are called such, because they can be witnessed throughout the continent of Africa regardless of the region or ethnicity. Additionally, the overwhelming majority of these movements are generally not witnessed in European traditional and/or folk dances. For example, torso contractions generally, and pelvic contractions specifically, are not witnessed in European folk dances. Another example of an African body movement that is not witnessed in European traditional or old-world dances would be the rapid successive circular movements of the head executed alone or within a dance step.[5] Steps are the building blocks of a dance; hence, a dance is comprised of a multitude of steps. Fittingly, when considering the above discussions on dance steps and body movements, it is clear that they can provide significant clues for determining appropriated steps and dances.

Movement vocabulary

The movement vocabulary of a dance is the specific steps that tell the story. All traditional African dances have meaning; thus, they all tell stories or contain narratives. Researchers, in their quest to interpret African dances, must read the movement vocabulary. Clues for understanding the movement vocabulary come from the dance system itself. All traditional African dances are microcosms of the culture they spring from. Accordingly, an understanding of the culture will provide greater comprehension of the dance system and by extension the movement vocabulary under study. It is noteworthy, however, that different dances reflect the culture in different ways. Some African dances may contain specific steps that tell the story, but some may be comprised of steps that are components of the story. In this latter category of dances, the dance must be considered as a whole – rather than assessing the steps individually – to ascertain the meaning that the movement vocabulary is attempting to disclose. As a general rule, it would be prudent to study the individual steps and the dance as a whole for a complete picture.

Notes

1 In contrast to acute torso angles, there are also obtuse torso angles where the torso is held at an angle greater than 90 degrees. Although the overwhelming majority of African and African diaspora dances employ acute angles, there are instances where dances are performed with obtuse torso angles. For example, the dance limbo, often witnessed in the island of Trinidad as well as other islands in the Caribbean, involves the backward bend (or obtuse angle) of the torso to maneuver under a stick held parallel to the ground while dancing.
2 See Abiola, *History Dances*, 40. Terms utilized in this study are specific to Afrikinesis and may not be identical to scientific terminology.
3 See Abiola, *History Dances*, 41.
4 Ibid., 66.
5 For a comparison between the folk/traditional dances of Africa and those of Europe, visit https://www.youtube.com/watch?v=HLVcO6y-fQE to observe a sample of 27 European folk dances.

4 Application of the Afrikinesis paradigm

The Afrikinesis paradigm values the lived and embodied experiences of individuals of the group, the group as a complete entity, the collective memories, and communal experiences of people of African descent. Use of this paradigm facilitates full comprehension of how the society's culture specifically and its history in general are inextricably bound to African and African diaspora dance. Therefore, at the onset of employing an Afrikinesis framework to a project, there should be an initial process and an initial understanding that the researcher should employ. The two terms that describe the process and the understanding are *observation* and *embodiment*, and they are significant for the most effective application of the Afrikinesis paradigm.

Simply defined, observation in the Afrikinesis paradigm is the act of witnessing or watching, and examination and perusal of the African and African diaspora dance as a whole, and the body movements individually, that the research is to be conducted on. One need not be a dance practitioner to properly observe the dances or body movements and accurately make assessments for the purpose of the research framework. There are two genres of observation: surface observation and in-depth observation. Surface observation reveals clearly recognizable phenomena such as an acute torso in the low position or a dance step described as characteristically African due to its rigorous employment of both the top parts and the bottom parts of the body simultaneously. Surface observations reveal the obvious. In-depth observation involves witnessing and identifying subtle, generally unnoticed, partially hidden, unexpected, or unconventional dance movements. False steps, false falls, partial contractions (torso and pelvic), syncopated dance movements, to name a few, fall under this category.

Embodiment has two meanings. With regard to African dance research, embodiment can infer that the researcher is a performer of the dances under study (a novice or an experienced dance practitioner), or the researcher is a person of African descent. Thus, embodiment, for the purposes of this study, denotes to embody the dance or to embody the heritage of Africa. Embodiment will affect the process for collecting the findings and the perception of the findings. Indeed, a practitioner will perceive the body movements that they are executing themselves in a distinct manner than someone who observes the body movements from the outside looking in. A person of African descent will perceive the history of Africa and the African diaspora in a manner informed by their experiences which will unavoidably be different than the perception of someone who is not of African descent. It is important to understand that different does not mean inaccurate nor does it mean unimportant. Research of this magnitude should be discussed from as many perspectives as possible. Hence, while proficient application of the Afrikinesis paradigm requires meticulous observation skills, embodiment itself is not a necessary requirement. The beauty of this paradigm is that it discloses previously omitted spheres of inquiry that are distinctly suited for African and African diaspora dance research; significant areas of inquiry that European research models do not generally consider or include. Thus, researchers who are not of African descent and who are not themselves African or African diaspora dance practitioners will be able to effectively utilize the Afrikinesis paradigm to conduct research on African and African diaspora dance. Although their lens will be different from researchers who are of African descent, researchers that are not of African descent and/or are not African dance practitioners will still be able to approach the research from a culturally and historically sensitive perspective. Hence, in this case, different does not mean wrong.

Application of the Afrikinesis paradigm requires that a dance under research can be identified as derived from or can contain elements of an African dance system. To test for this requirement, the dance must contain one or more of the elements in the characteristically African body movement category, and one or more items in the African aesthetic group. Some dances, such as those borrowed and those appropriated from people of African descent by others, may only exhibit characteristically African body movements, but they may be divorced from the other aspects of the African dance aesthetic. For example, African dance body movements incorporated into a European-American modern dance may no longer exhibit a relationship between the lived experiences of peoples of African descent in a given society. However, the specific African body movements would still be able to be identified and claimed as African due to the fact that characteristically African body movements comprise both the African aesthetic and the characteristically African category.

Indigenous traditional African dances are obviously of African origin. Hence, the Afrikinesis paradigm would not be utilized to identify the obvious origin of the dance movements. Rather, the paradigm would be utilized for countless other inquiries and functions. For example, the Afrikinesis paradigm would facilitate the incorporation of structure into the research process. The paradigm would provide an organized approach to the research and facilitate proficiency through a more organic, authentic, and realistic outcome. It facilitates deeper understanding of African cultural tenets and the capacity to experience dance and its research through African lenses. The result of utilizing the Afrikinesis framework is enhanced understanding and richer

Application of the Afrikinesis paradigm 31

narratives. The Afrikinesis paradigm provides a lens through which to examine African and African diaspora dance and provides rich cultural information that general frameworks often miss. Let us consider a few case studies where an Afrikinesis framework is utilized for research on African dance systems and African diaspora dance systems.

Afrikinesis paradigm at work: bomba, the Afro-Puerto Rican dance

The African descent population of the island of Puerto Rico performs an African diaspora dance known as bomba. To situate bomba in an Afrikinesis paradigm, the dance movements, dance system, aesthetic, and the relationship between the dance and the community it hails from must be observed and analyzed. It is best to observe and scrutinize the body movements of the dance first. The movement vocabulary of bomba includes steps that are characteristically African. Dancers employ torso contractions, hip movements from right to left, simultaneous diverse body movements, which employ parts of the body above and below the waist and others. Bomba also contains location-specific African dance movements such as the pauses witnessed in West African dances, and the dancer–drummer relationship where the drummer accents the dancer's body movements with improvised and traditional drumbeats and rhythms. This relationship, also known as the dancer–drummer bond, between the drummer and dancer is witnessed in Mandinka dances of the Senegambia region of West Africa, among others.[1]

Bomba is also practiced within a dance system. Thus, the drummers must have knowledge of specific rhythms for the dance, there are distinct drums used for bomba, the color of the attire that the women wear has meaning and the attire (extremely flared skirts) itself is also used by the women dancers to communicate dance narratives to drummers and to add emphasis on the movements. The action of incorporating the rhythmic movements applied to flared skirts within a dance is akin to raising one's voice in speech or placing emphasis on a word or phrase to accentuate its importance. There are historic locations associated with the origin of bomba and its authentic practice, and so on.[2] Subsequently, the drum rhythms, the drummers themselves, the dance attire, dance movements, and the location where the dance is traditionally practiced all facilitate conveyance of the dance message and therefore comprise the dance system.

The culture of the drums and the word to describe them forms a significant part of the dance system.[3] The word "bomba" is used to denote the dance and the drum among the Afro-Puerto Rican dance community. This practice is similar to many African cultural traditions. For instance, in the Central and West Central African language Kikongo, the word "ngoma" is used to denote particular dances, events, and drum rhythms. In Swahili, a language spoken in East, Central, and Central-East Africa, the word "ngoma" describes the drums themselves, the dance, and the music. Musicians that master the bomba drum are called a bombero, which is comparable to the practice of calling djembe drum players djembefola, in the Mandinka drum culture.

In addition to knowledge of traditional rhythms played for the dance, bomba drummers must know the difference between the drums and the function of each. For example, the *buleador* drum keeps the constant rhythm. It sets the pace for the dance and assures that the pace is maintained throughout. The *primo* is a lead drum (also referred to as *el seguidor*). Its drummer follows the dancer and accents the steps the dancer is executing. The drummer playing the *primo* drum utilizes their improvisational skills to highlight and accent the steps and body movements of the dancer. These traditions are similar to the drum and dance traditions of the Mandinka in the Senegambia region of West Africa.[4] When the communication between the dancer and the drummer playing accents of the dancer's movements on the *primo* drum are effectively performed, spectators from the community will shout the word "speak," denoting acknowledgment of the conversation. All of the aforementioned aspects of the dance system including the participation of the spectators, ties the bomba dance traditions to historical cultural tenets in Africa, while reflecting current tenets in African diaspora dance. This practice addresses the second and third criteria for identifying the African aesthetic in African diaspora dance. The second criterion requires that the dance display current culture while simultaneously housing and displaying dance history. The third criterion states that the dance should also exhibit a relationship between the dance system and the lived experiences of the people in the community.

The African diaspora within Africa: Gnawa dance and the Afrikinesis paradigm

The next example of how to apply the Afrikinesis framework and methodology to an African diaspora dance system will involve an analysis of the Gnawa dance system. Ethnic groups that are indigenous to North Africa (from west to central) and the Sahara Desert are historically known as Haratin, Amazigh, and Tuareg, among others.[5] The Gnawa are another ethnic group that resides in North Africa. They were forcibly transported to North Africa via the trans-Saharan slave trade centuries ago. Historically, the Gnawa originated in countries in the Western Sahel and south of the Sahara Desert including, Mali, Guinea, Senegal, Gambia, and Guinea Bissau, among others. Accordingly, the predominant ethnic groups that the Gnawa are comprised of include Mandinka (also known as Mandingo), Fulani, Wolof, Serer, Susu, Bambara, Hausa, among others.[6] The culture of the Gnawa reflects Sahelian, West, and North African culture. Syncretism is also at work where the culture of Islam and authentic African culture are synchronized. Gnawa dance systems reveal rich narratives and situating research of such dance systems

Application of the Afrikinesis paradigm 33

within an Afrikinesis paradigm will facilitate deeper understanding of the findings. Accordingly, the Gnawa dance system as it is practiced in Morocco is the next sample case study.

As discussed earlier, the first task to be performed for utilization of the Afrikinesis paradigm is to observe the dance system, step, body movement, or specific dance under study. Surface observation should occur to aid in the identification of what are and are not characteristically African body movements or location-specific African body movements. The second task is to perform an in-depth observation. In-depth observations should be conducted to provide rich narratives that will facilitate meaningful conceptualization of the dance system. The comprehension of and appropriate application of the Afrikinesis paradigm for research on Gnawa dance is vital due to the large presence of syncretism and the resulting non-African influences in this dance system. Due to historic invasions (European and Arab), colonization, and cultural hegemony, there are Islamic (Arab), Andalusian (Spanish), and French influences in Moroccan culture.[7] Accordingly, these influences can also be witnessed in portions of Gnawa dance systems.

Surface observation followed by in-depth observation reveal that many body movements and dance steps in the Gnawa dance system are African at their core. Gnawa dances contain characteristically African body movements such as simultaneous diverse body movements. For example, a dancer will twirl their head in a circular motion to initiate and maintain the circular movement of a tassel attached to the top of their fez (a felt cylindrical hat with a black tassel attached to the top) while they execute swift foot movements and kicks while they play qraqebs or castanets with each of their hands. Another instance of diverse simultaneous African body movements is when the Gnawa dancer executes swift kicks and percussive foot movements, drops to one knee and subtly moves or sways the back, wriggles the shoulders, and/ or moves the head in circular movements.

The instruments, attire, music, and circumstance with which the dances occur must also be engaged to gain insight into the significance of Gnawa dance. As such, analysis of an individual body movement or one dance step will not suffice for our purposes; the dance system as a whole must be considered. The music is a significant aspect of the Gnawa dance system. The predominant instruments used are the gimbri (also known as the sinter or the hajuj), the qraqeb (also known as the krakeb, or karkab, among other names), and the tbel (also known as the ganga).[8] The gimbri is a lute with three strings and is played by plucking. The qraqebs are long metal castanets. They are often played while executing dance movements. The tbel is a drum with a skin attached to both sides. It is played with one straight stick and one curved stick. The drummer observes the dancer and plays accents on the drum to accentuate the dancer's movements. Through this process, the dancer and the drummer forge a bond, and each is able to anticipate what the other will do; hence, a dancer–drummer bond is formed.[9] As discussed earlier, the dancer–drummer bond is also witnessed in countless Mandinka dance systems practiced in the Sahel region of West Africa among others. Hence, the dancer–drummer bond is a location-specific historically African practice.

With regard to the circumstances with which the dances occur, the Gnawa also practice a spiritual dance–music-driven ritualistic event known as the lila.[10] It is founded on the dances and songs of Gnawa historical past and the spiritual systems they brought with them from African locations south of the Sahara Desert. Songs describe their slave ancestors, their lands of origin in Mali, Senegal, Gambia, and so on, the traditional African culture that they have retained, African ethnic groups that they are comprised of, and so on. Similar to West African Yoruba and Akan spiritual ceremonies, the Gnawan lila is buttressed upon spiritual trances or spirit possession accessed through dance.[11] For example, the practice of entering trance (or possession) through dance is witnessed when practitioners of the Yoruba religion seek possession by the Orishas, or the emissaries of Olodumare, the Supreme God. Another example is the act of becoming possessed by the Abosom through dance practiced in the Akan spiritual systems of Ghana and the Ivory Coast. Trance provides a means through which the saints in the Gnawa lilas, the Orishas in the Yoruba system, and the Abosom in Akan spirituality can communicate with their patrons. Dance is not only utilized to enter the trance state, but it is also used to express the particular spirit or saint, its characteristics, its worldview, and the advice or warnings it wishes to convey to the participants at the lila. This practice of dancing into a trance and convening with the saints is a direct carryover from African cultural systems practiced for time immemorial by Africans south of the Saharan Desert. However, one need not guess where the spiritual dance traditions of the lilas originated, their origins are disclosed by the Gnawas in the songs that accompany the dances. During the lila, participant engagement with those in trance or spiritually possessed is also similar to that of the Yoruba and the Akan spiritual systems.

Gnawa dress

In accordance with the Afrikinesis paradigm, the attire worn by the practitioners of the dances under study is part of the dance system and thus, must be engaged. The attire of the Gnawa is distinct from all other ethnic groups in Morocco. The most striking element of Gnawa dress is the copious use of cowrie shells on their garments and hats. Cowrie shells are also used to decorate Gnawa instruments. The use of cowrie shells in this manner is not historically practiced by any other ethnic group in Morocco. The cowrie shells signify identity with their original homelands in the Sahel and in West Africa, where cowries were used as adornment, currency, and as talismans for spiritual rituals and ceremonies, among other things.[12]

Application of the Afrikinesis paradigm 35

Women and dance among the Gnawa

Lilas are an organized, deliberate spiritual event. Participants in attendance are meticulously selected to attend by the organizer. Most often, the organizer or host of the lila is a woman. Women are also often the muqadma or the medium or shaman who communicates with the saint and conveys the thoughts of the saints to the people. The muqadma has advanced knowledge of all the saints, their specific dances and characteristics, the attire associated with them, their distinct colors, chants, songs, and specific practices, and so on. Lilas generally involve dancing all night and into the next day, and women are usually the muqadmas executing the dances. In Morocco, men are witnessed displaying secular dances in public. Women often run the sacred dancing that is not open to public or uninvited eyes.[13] The practice of separating the performance and roles of dances by gender is witnessed throughout Africa south of the Sahara in rites of passage rituals and ceremonies among others.

The Gnawa as a diasporic community: a special case

It is paramount that researchers engage in the history, theory, and study of African diaspora dance in an effort to understand what the African diaspora is beyond the generic and only partially accurate definition, "people of African descent living outside of the continent of Africa." In the twenty-first century, hundreds of millions of people of African descent live outside of Africa and the numbers increase annually. Even so, the aforementioned definition is still lacking depth of understanding. The word "diaspora" is defined as the dispersal or spread of a people from their original homeland. There is no stipulation indicating where the dispersed are spread, and only that the spread of people is away from their original homeland. To add more context, African diasporans are linked together through the innate retention and celebration of their African culture and heritage whether they are aware of such or not. In other words, the African diaspora is comprised of people dispersed from their original homeland, who innately carry with them their original African culture, and passes it down through their generations. Consciousness of this practice is a nonfactor. They are subsequently bonded together by the culture and heritage that they share. Distinctions based on different environments, types of subjugation, enslavements, the colonization styles of different oppressive governments may exist, but the universal commonalities within their African heritage far outweigh the distinctions. Accordingly, the African diaspora is considered one region, though it is comprised of countless countries and islands throughout the world. Fittingly, the Gnawa recognizes that they are a part of the African diaspora. The Gnawa were involuntarily transported or dispersed, from their original homelands south of the Sahara Desert. They were transported across the Desert via the trans-Saharan slave trade to unknown lands in North Africa. As such, they qualify as African diasporans. In addition to the forced migration overall, there are similarities to specific aspects of the forced migration experienced by enslaved Africans during the transatlantic slave trade. The horrors experienced while traveling across the Sahara Desert, and the unprecedented deaths that resulted from the journey are comparable to the atrocious experiences of enslaved Africans of the transatlantic slave trade while crossing the Atlantic Ocean. This part of that perilous journey is known as the "middle passage." Indeed, the horrendous and often fatal journey across the Sahara Desert is sometimes also referred to as the middle passage as well.[14]

The West African dance dununba through an Afrikinesis lens

Thus far, African diaspora dance systems have been utilized for examples of how the Afrikinesis paradigm can be used to position African-oriented dance research within a theoretically organized framework. With respect to African diaspora dances, the paramount concern is usually identifying the dance, or portions of it as African in origin. Therefore, conversations about surface and in-depth observational findings generally occupy a significant portion of the discourse on the research on African diaspora dance. Once the African origins have been systematically established, the study can focus on the African aesthetic and other aspects of the research. However, at this juncture, the traditional dance dununba (also referred to as dundunba), a dance that is historically African, will serve as the next example.

Dununba is a dance practiced by the Mandinka in the Senegambia region of West Africa and parts of the Western Sahel.[15] Its origin is Hamana, Guinea, and the word dununba, refers to the dance and the drum rhythms that accompany it. Dununba belongs to the family of dances in the overarching genre of rite of passage dances. Historically, in virtually all regions of Africa, all prepubescent boys and girls were required to pass through the rite of passage process. Participants progressed through the different stages or grades with peers in their age group range.[16] These peer groups were bonded for life. Through the rite of passage process, participants learned how to be responsible citizens in their communities and to make valuable contributions to their societies. Lessons were either taught and learned through the dance system or validated through a ceremony driven by dance.[17] Dununba was a dance that was used by a rite of passage peer group, usually a younger group of men, to discard or change perceived outdated behaviors, rituals, and so on, still practiced by older rite of passage male peer groups. It was danced to challenge a person or group. Subsequently, dununba was known as the dance of the "strong men." The dance included a distinctive root step that indubitably denoted assertion, strength, as well as distinctive pants worn by the male dancers with an extremely low-lying crotch. The rhythms for dununba are numerous – roughly 30 or more – but the dance steps, body movements, and movement vocabulary remain the same regardless of which dununba rhythms are played. Historically, the performance of dununba included extraordinary feats such as chewing glass and stick flogging. Today, such feats are not practiced, though the meaning of the dance has not changed.[18]

Although it is traditionally a men's dance, eventually, women were incorporated into the dununba dance system, and dance steps and body movements devised specifically for women were also incorporated into the corpus of dance movements associated with dununba. It is noteworthy that presently, women also perform the male dununba steps, along with the traditional head gesture and other body gestures or movement vocabularies associated with the root step.[19]

It is already understood that dununba is a dance that originated in Africa. The application of both a surface and an in-depth observation will confirm this fact. Accordingly, the purpose of situating dununba within the Afrikinesis paradigm is not to ascertain whether the dance or its movements are of African origin. The dance possesses myriad body movements that can be categorized as characteristically African and location-specific African body movements. Hence, the purpose for utilizing an Afrikinesis paradigm for research on an African dance such as dununba is to obtain an extensive understanding of the meanings of the narrative that the dance is conveying and its relationship with and impact on the performers, spectators and culture, to uncover unknown tenets or unexplored or under-research tenets of the culture of the society it hails from, and so on. The Afrikinesis paradigm informs researchers of the questions that they should be asking and the often-overlooked phenomena they should be seeking answers for.

As an example, the second criterion of the African dance aesthetic discussed in Chapter 2, is that the dance display current culture while simultaneously housing and displaying dance history. The incorporation of women into the dance dununba reflects the current developments of Guinean society with regard to women. Dununba is a dance that is performed to challenge old mores and perceived outdated practices. Guinea, after independence, was one of the first African polities to challenge the practice of female genital mutilation (FGM).[20] The practice of FGM was consequently not condoned by the new Guinean government. Subsequently, utilizing the Afrikinesis paradigm forces one to look deeper into the narratives that the dance under study is seeking to convey. Moreover, the incorporation of women's steps into dununba also satisfies the African dance aesthetic criterion of a dance reflecting current cultural tenets while simultaneously exhibiting cultural history within the dance. Historically, the rhythms, male's dance steps, and attire remain the same in current executions of dununba. Yet the presence of women in all aspects of this historically men's dance displays present cultural developments, and the execution of the dance ties the historic narratives to the current cultural developments simultaneously.

The current presentation of the dance dununba with the inclusion of women is the result of lived experiences of women in general, and of men who experienced FGM through their sisters, wives, mothers, and so on. Indeed, many of the dununba dances executed as a part of a dance ensemble performance and as part of its repertory, are choreographed by men. Utilizing an Afrikinesis framework would first require in-depth observation to identify these often-overlooked tenets and then to unpack them.

It is also notable that distinct dununba body movements are described as historic in this study to avoid confusion. In this sense, historic denotes dance practices that have been developed in the distant past. Tradition, on the other hand, can be historic, but can also be newly created or recently altered. Hence, the original, older dununba steps initially performed solely by men are understood to be historic. The current dununba steps executed by women are more recent, but have been passed down for at least three generations, which satisfies the requirements for them to now be a tradition. As time passes, the women's dununba dance movements will also become historic. An Afrikinesis framework provides the researcher with the insight to know to address such tenets, rather than relegating them to the realm of insignificance and allowing them to go unnoticed.

Notes

1 See Abiola, *History Dances*, 55, for a detailed description of the dancer-drummer bond.
2 Today, bomba is performed in diverse locations in Puerto Rico, other Caribbean islands, and in the United States. However, historically, bomba's center of origin was Loíza, Santurce, Mayagüez, and Ponce.
3 See Juan Cartagena, "When Bomba Becomes the National Music of the Puerto Rico Nation . . . ," *Centro Journal* XVI, no. 1 (2004).
4 See Abiola, *History Dances*, 51–53.
5 Tuaregs and Amazighs (or Imazighen, plural) are also referred to as Berbers, a derogatory term. As such, this work will not use the term Berber in any of the discussions in this work. The Haratin are Black people that are indigenous to Morocco, but whose position as one of the original inhabits of the country is not fully acknowledged by the government. To learn more about their history, see Ghouki El Hamel, *Black Morocco: A History of Slavery, Race, and Islam* (Cambridge: Cambridge University Press, 2013), 103–13.
6 The Sahel is a semi-arid region on the continent of Africa that separates the Sahara Desert from the tropical regions in the central and south. It extends across the continent of Africa from the Atlantic coast in the West to the Red Sea in the East. The Sahel comprises ten countries, Mauritania, Senegal, Gambia, Mali, Burkino Faso, Niger, Nigeria, Chad, Sudan, and Eritrea.
7 These are oversimplifications for centuries-old influences. The syncretistic nature of each of these influences will not be discussed here to avert a large digression. However, it is important to note that Andalusian culture is comprised of North African Moorish culture and Spanish culture. Although Islam originated in the Middle East, when it migrated to Africa through Arab invasions, trade, and so on, it was not practiced in its pure state universally in Africa. Many African states, polities, and communities combined African traditional religious systems and African secular practices with Islam. Africanized Islam was the result and is still practiced in countless localities in Africa currently.

8 There are diverse spellings for the Gnawa themselves and the instruments they play.
9 The dancer-drummer bond is an aspect of African diaspora dance systems that has been retained in countless African diaspora dance communities.
10 See Christopher Witulski, "Negotiated Authenticity within Morocco's Gnawa Ritual," *Ethnomusicology* 62, no. 1 (Winter 2018), https://www.jstor.org/stable/10.5406/ethnomusicology.62.1.0058.
11 The Yoruba are an ethnic group in Nigeria, West Africa. They can also be found in Benin and Togo. For more information on Yoruba ritualistic practices particularly with respect to dance see Omofolabo S. Ajayi, "Chapter 2: Dance in Religious Communication," in *Yoruba Dance: The Semiotics of Movement and Body Attitude in a Nigerian Culture* (Trenton: Africa World Press, Inc., 1998). The Akan are an ethnic group in Ghana and the Ivory Coast in West Africa. For general understanding of Akan religion see Anthony Epherim-Donkor, *African Personality and Spirituality: The Role of Abosom and Human Essence* (Lanham: Lexington Books, 2016). The Yoruba religion is also practiced in the diaspora outside of the African continent. The Akan religion is as well but with smaller numbers of practitioners. For more information on the lila, see Maisie Sum, "Music for the Unseen: Interaction Between Two Realms During a Gnawa Lila," *African Music* 9, no. 3 (2013), https://www.jstor.org/stable/24877319.
12 Cowrie shells were utilized for myriad purposes in Africa, from the west coast to the east coast south of the Sahara Desert. In addition to adornment, they were used as currency.
13 See Cynthia J. Becker, *Blackness in Morocco: Gnawa Identity through Music and Visual Culture* (Minneapolis: University of Minnesota Press, 2020), 66. In her book, Becker describes numerous instances where she was invited to lilas but was asked not to photograph the women at the lila ceremonies.
14 See John Wright, *The Trans-Saharan Slave Trade* (London: Routledge, 2007). Wright discusses the trans-Saharan slave trade and includes points of comparisons between it and aspects of the transatlantic slave trade including the reasons why the passage across the Sahara Desert was similar to the middle passage across the Atlantic Ocean during the transatlantic slave trade.
15 The Mandinka are also known as Mandingo, Malinke, Manding, and so on. The designation is contingent upon the region's dialect and language. For example, in the Senegambia region, Mandinka is the preferred designation, but in Guinea and its surrounding areas, Malinke is the preferred name. The Sahel is a transitional section on the continent of Africa where the Sahara Desert ends, and the environment begins its transition to become tropical. The Sahel is that transition. It is characterized by grassland and includes areas of woodlands and shrublands. It is not completely tropical nor is it completely desert. The Western Sahel includes Northern Senegal, Southern Mauritania, Central Mali, and Northern Burkina Faso.
16 Rite of passage is also known as age grades. See Abiola, *History Dances*, 12–13.
17 Ceremonies driven by dance are ceremonies where the dance itself contains the message that is to be conveyed. The body movements, props, attire, songs, and so on, are the conveyers of the message, hence, no spoken words are needed.
18 In the African dance ballet titled "Jubilee," performed by Les Ballets Africains, the performers danced dununba to challenge an unscrupulous general that the village wanted to leave. A ballet tells a story through dance. See *The 50 Years Golden "Jubilee,"* Les Ballets Africains. DVD (2004) McFarland & Company Inc., Publishers, WI: World Music Productions.
19 Although women now perform the men's dununba dance steps, it is curious that I have never witnessed men performing the women's dununba steps. Currently, women have also been witnessed wearing the men's dununba pants while performing the dance.

20 In addition to parts of Africa, Female Genital Mutilation, or FGM, is practiced in Arab states, Eastern Europe, Latin America, India and other parts of Asia, among other locations. FGM is the practice of deliberately cutting, removing, changing, or injuring a female's genitals for non-medical reasons. There are no health benefits to FGM. It is a painful procedure that can cause serious harm to women and girls physically and psychologically, and in some cases it has caused death. For an inspirational story of how a Kenyan woman defied the nefarious tradition of FGM and saved the lives of countless other women, see Nice Lang'ete, *The Girls in the Wild Fig Tree: How I Fought to Save Myself, My Sister, and Thousands of Girls Worldwide* (New York: Little, Brown and Company, 2021). To learn more about FGM in general, see Rosemarie Skaine, *Female Genital Mutilation: Legal, Cultural and Medical Issues* (Jefferson: McFarland & Company Inc., Publishers, 2005). Please note that FGM occurs in many locations throughout the world. Many authors on the topic present the subject as though it only occurs in Africa, or it occurs mostly in Africa and sparsely in other parts of the world.

5 A synergistic union
Afrikinesis and African dance research

The utilization of a research framework suited specifically to the study of African and African diaspora dance is not the end of the research journey. The research findings resulting from such a model must be accessible and widely distributed. The idea of accessibility refers more to presentation of research findings than to format. Clearly, research documented in books is the most accessible to a wide range of readers, since journal subscriptions, access to libraries, and so on are not required. Yet accessibility here is referring to how the research is presented within its own document. Is the language and document formatting comprehensible to non-academics and laymen as well as scholars? Or is the information conveyed impeded or ladened by jargon and discourse incomprehensible to those outside of the field? Information on, knowledge of, and research on African and African diaspora dance have historically been omitted from the cannons of academia and the literature of non-specialists alike. Consequently, the voices of Africana (African and African diaspora) communities have been unheard at best and erased at worst. The gravity of this phenomenon cannot be overstated. Africana dance often houses narratives and experiences that are not recorded elsewhere. For instance, the jalis of the Senegambian polities of Mali, Guinea, Senegal, and Gambia, among others, are an integral part of the culture.[1] The jalis retain generations and often centuries of histories in their minds. They impart their knowledge to audiences through songs, chants, and dance. Although jalis witnessed presently are overwhelmingly men, historically, women were also jalis. In Captain Theophilus Conneau's 1853 eyewitness account, he described the versatility and skill of a female jali as she plays balafon, the traditional instrument of the jali class, and dances:

> This was something like a harmonica: a board the size of a tea waiter with a light open frame at the extreme ends. On the frame were tied two strings made of cane, and on it reposed several pieces of bamboo well cleaned from the pith. These pieces were gradually made, one larger than the other, declining in size and placed in rotation; under them were placed seven

gourds also gradually declining in size. This instrument was carried with a strap around the neck and played with two wooden hammers covered with gutta-percha. Its harmony was peculiar. The female musician who played it had fastened to her elbows, wrists, ankles, and knees a lot of bells which she managed to sound as she struck the harmonica and danced in the meantime.[2]

Rather than relying solely on scarce historic eyewitness accounts such as Captain Conneau's, there are other clues regarding the female practice of the jali profession hidden in plain sight in the dance of the jali, lamban. The full name of the dance is lamban jalidon, which means "lamban dance of the jali" in the Mandinka language. Lamban was created by the jali class in Mali for the jali class.[3] It was created by women and was historically and still presently is performed primarily by women. Men were incorporated more recently which is evident by the limited number of steps performed by men and the simplicity of the steps. In lamban, the women's steps are plentiful which denotes advanced age along with their complexity.[4] The clues that provide evidence that the jali profession historically included women exist in the dance system of the jali but are not widely documented. Clues such as Captain Conneau's account are scarce and not broadly accessible as they are housed in specific archives or manuscript collections. Much of the time the discovery of such narratives is serendipitous. Situating African dance research within the Afrikinesis paradigm exposes this rich narrative because the dance or body movement itself becomes the primary source. Within the Afrikinesis paradigm, both surface and in-depth observations, and application of the African dance aesthetic will provide a prolific amount of information about the dance, its history, practitioners, and so on.

In Mali, the profession of the jali is protected and guaranteed to endure via schools established specifically to monitor and advance the profession. However, there are vast areas of the continent of Africa with cultures that do not contain jalis. For example, the Jola of the Senegambia region of West Africa do not have jalis in their culture.[5] As such, their history is recorded in their dances. For example, the dance sofora was created to bring all the Jola clans from diverse locations in Senegambia together at a specified location. Before sofora existed, the Jola gathered together once every ten years. It was determined by the elders that ten years was tool long between reunions. Thus, the dance system sofora was created to reunite the Jolas every year.

Contrary to the notion that indigenous writing systems and therefore written primary sources are scarce in Africa, there are myriad cultures in Africa that created their own unique writing systems in which the dances of their culture could be recorded. In addition to the popularly known hieroglyphics of Egypt in Northeast Africa, other indigenous scripts exist in other parts of the continent. For example, there is the Amharic script in Ethiopia, the Mende script in Sierra Leone, the Bassa script in Liberia, the Meroitic script of Sudan, the Nsibidi script in Nigeria and Cameroon, the Shumom script of Cameroon, and the Adinkra symbols of Ghana, among others.[6] But what if a script has fallen prey to abandonment such as the ancient scripts of the Kpelle, Gola, Lorma, and Kissi ethnic groups? How would the narratives and history after the writing system have fallen into disuse be recorded? Additionally, there are African scripts that have yet to be deciphered such as the Meroitic script of Sudan. What of the societies in Africa without indigenous scripts and without professional jalis? The good news is the history, culture, and current social developments of societies that are embedded in the dances of Africa. It is noteworthy that most African cultures that do possess indigenous scripts still record their cultural history in dance systems as well. Thus, dance research that utilizes an African dance-oriented framework has the capacity to reveal lived experiences not previously documented, experiences that are not discussed in other sources, and fill in gaps in knowledge in existing dance sources.

When African dances traveled across the Atlantic Ocean via the transatlantic slave trade, the Sahara Desert due to the trans-Sahara slave trade, the Red Sea or the Indian Ocean as a result of the East African slave trade, the African worldview, the culture, history, and experiences of African people arrived at diverse locations across the world. The dances and their distinctly African body movements were retained through generations. In addition to the historic narratives that the dances arrived with, they were clothed in the experiences of the African descended people in these diverse locations over a span of centuries.

African dance systems, whole or in part, and African body movements witnessed in dances in the diaspora are warehouses of knowledge. There is a constant, ever-flowing cultural conversation throughout Africa, and between Africa and her diaspora. This cultural interchange is sometimes obvious, but it is often veiled or unnoticed. Indeed, the outgrowth of hip hop dancing from breakdancing to rap music, which emanates from the oral traditions of West Africa to the dance styles of krumping and twerking among others, retain the initial seeds of meaning. As a result, the narratives of lived experiences within African-oriented dances are told, retold, adapted, reshaped, edited, and subsequently experienced by all who engage them. Accordingly, in addition to the facilitation of immersion in the African diaspora experience, when utilizing an Afrikinesis paradigm, cultural appropriation of that experience is also averted. As such, cultural appropriation is thwarted by decisive documentation and incontrovertible substantiation. Both are achieved when thorough research practices are married to a research model that was created specifically for the particular phenomenon under study. Afrikinesis, then, is the perfect paradigm and methodology to capture ancient and current accounts, identify and reclaim appropriated narratives and body movements, and interpret previously undeciphered interpretations in African and African diaspora dances and body movements.

Notes

1 A jali (also spelled jeli, djali, and djeli) is a historian, poet, singer responsible for memorizing generations and oftentimes centuries of historical information. The jail reveals the information through spoken word, chanting, or song, with the accompaniment of music. The differences in spelling represents regional variations in pronunciation.
2 For the complete account, see Captain Theophilus Conneau, *A Slaver's Log Book or 20 Years' Residence in Africa* (Englewood: Prentice-Hall, Inc., Reprint 1976 [1854]), 131. In his journal, Conneau describes his experiences with dance and music in the Senegambian region of Africa. The instrument described in Captain Conneau's account is a balafon (comparable to a wooden xylophone).
3 Often dance systems in Africa were created for specific audiences. For instance, there are rite of passage dances that were created to teach initiates specific life lessons, and rite of passage dances created to celebrate the achievement of completion for those who graduated from the rite of passage process. In the case of the former, the dances are performed in private with the initiates and their mentors as the intended audience, while the latter dance is performed publicly for the entire community to witness and celebrate. The jali dance lamban, was initially created by the jali class specifically for an audience of jalis.
4 See Abiola, *History Dances*, 66–67. In Mandinka dance systems, complex or sophisticated dance steps denote age. Such steps require and array of complex body movements and often include false falls or false steps, pauses in movement, syncopated steps, and so on. In Mandinka dance systems, an abundance of steps witnessed in one dance also denotes age. Similar to geneticists' convention of determining advanced age by observing the abundance of diversity evident in DNA or the practice of linguists determining the increased age of languages based on an abundance of words to describe a single phenomenon, in Mandinka dance systems and abundance of steps in a single dance indicates advanced age. In Mandinka dance systems, a wealth of steps witnessed in one dance indicates that the dance has been around long enough for steps to be added to the original steps, for those new steps to become tradition, and for more steps to be added to them, and for those steps to become tradition, and so on. It must be noted that a tradition is created by passing down cultural phenomena through generations. In addition to *History Dances*, see Chapter 3 in this study for a detailed discussion of African dance steps and body movements.
5 The Jola also known as Ajamat is an ethnic group located in Senegal, Gambia, and Guinea-Bissau, West Africa.
6 For a discussion on indigenous African writing systems, see Million Meshesha and C.V. Jawahar, "Indigenous Scripts of African Languages," *Indilinga African Journal of Indigenous Knowledge Systems* 6, no. 2 (May 15, 2007).

Appendix

To fully understand and engage the narratives of African and African diaspora dance, each dance must be approached as a system. The dance itself comprises only a small portion of the copious elements employed to tell the dance's story and to access the dance's knowledge. Subsequently, all items, comments, and questions in Table A must be considered when conducting research on Africana dances. However, Table A is not exhaustive. In addition, all elements in Table A may not have a specific meaning.

Table A The Dance System

	The Dance System
The dance	- What is the meaning and purpose of the dance?
- What is the pace of the dance (is the dance performed slow or fast?)
- What is/are the gender(s) of the dancer(s)?
- Are circles or other patterns utilized in the performance of the dance?
- Which body movements are employed prolifically, scarcely, or not at all?
- Is the dance performed to music or without music?
- If performed to music, what kind of instruments are used?
- What is/are the gender(s) of the musicians?
- Is the dance performed in public or private?
- Who are the spectators and are they spectator-dancers?[1]
- Is the dance performed fully clothed, partially clothed, or naked?
- Is the dance traditional, historic, or was it recently created?
Attire	- What is the color of the attire?
- What is the cultural significance of the attire's color?
- What materials is the attire is comprised of – cotton, raffia, metals, leather, etc.?
- What is the cultural significance of the materials the attire is comprised of?
- What is the attire of the dancers?
- What is the attire of the musicians?
- Are masks or masquerade attire employed?
- If masks are employed, what is their significance?
- If masquerade attire, is it full body masquerade attire or partially?

(*Continued*)

Table A (Continued)

	The Dance System
Location	• The significance of the environment – the dance is performed in rural, city, village, secret, public, indoors, outdoors, etc.
Instruments	• What kind of instruments are utilized for the dance performance – drums, string instruments, wind instruments, a combination, lack of instruments, balafon, etc.? • Do dancers play instruments during their dance performance in addition to musicians? • What is the cultural significance of the specific instruments utilized? • Does hand clapping accompany music played on instruments or is the hand clapping the only instruments used?
Musicians	• Which types of musicians do the dance utilize – drummers, kora players, balafon players, flutists, etc.? • Do the musicians dance? • Do the musicians communicate with the dancers during the dance performance with their instruments? • Do the dancers respond to the musicians' communications with dance movements?
Props	• Are props used to enhance the dance, the dance message, or the music?[2] • What materials are the props made of? • What is the overall cultural significance of the props? • Are the props a specific color? • What is the cultural significance of the color of the props? • Masks, staffs, handheld props, environmental props (decorated trees, etc.) • Animals • Carvings • Stilts • Fire
Performers	• Who are the performers of the dance – women, men, children, elders, adolescents, masquerade dancers, rite of passage initiates, the uninitiated, etc.?
Time of year/day	• Is the dance performed during the rainy season, harvest, winter, or summer? • Is the dance performed at the time of year that a specific ceremony or ritual is to take place? • Is the dance performed at night, in the afternoon, in the morning, etc.? • Is the dance performed annually, biannually, monthly, weekly, etc.?
Color scheme	• Is there a particular color scheme that is prominent among the attire, props, instruments, environmental décor, etc.? • What is the cultural significance of the color scheme or lack thereof?

	The Dance System
Songs	• Is a song sung before, during, or after the dance is performed? • What is the cultural significance of the song? • Is the song ever sung without the performance of the dance? Why or why not? • If no song is sung during, before or after the dance, what is the cultural significance of the absence of a song? • Is music played before, during, or after the song is sung? • Who is singing – the dancers, the musicians, the spectators, rite of passage initiates, non-initiates, women, men, adolescents, children, elders, etc.?
Spectators	• Who is watching the dance – general public, rite of passage initiates, elders, peers, men, women, children, tourists, etc.?

Notes

1 The term spectator-dancers describes the cyclical positioning of audience members who watch the dance as a spectator, and then enters the dance as a performer, and ends the interaction by returning to the audience as a spectator once again. Many traditional secular dances performed in the Senegambia region allows for spectator-dancer interactions. See Abiola, *History Dances*, 75.
2 The Jola (spelled Djola in French) also known as the Ajamat, is an ethnic group in The Gambia, Senegal, and Guinea-Bissau, West Africa. In the Jola dance tradition, clackers are used to enhance the execution of the dance and to accompany the music. Clackers are held in each hand. They are made by carving blocks of wood that fit comfortably in the hand but still allows enough of it to be exposed to be hit against the clacker in the other hand. The sound made by the clackers enhances the traditional drumming for the dance. The sound that the clackers make is polyrhythmic.

Quick reference glossary

Acute torso To hold the top part of the body, over the waist, at an acute or less than an angle of 90° to the floor while executing a dance movement.

African aesthetic Historic and traditional African and African diaspora dances exhibit an African aesthetic. To exhibit an African aesthetic, the dance under study must include movements that are characteristically African, it should display current culture while simultaneously housing and displaying dance history, and there should be a relationship between the dance system and the lived experiences of the people in the community.

African diaspora The African diaspora is comprised of people dispersed from their original homeland, who innately carry with them their original African heritage and culture, and passes it down through their generations.

Afrikinesis A research paradigm and a methodology for research on African dance and African-oriented dance styles. The term "Afrikinesis" is a compilation of two words, "Afri" from the word African and "kinesis" which is defined as body movement. The author coined this designation for this paradigm, because it describes the most basic element in a dance, the movement of the body, and it identifies the people and the location of focus. Hence, the word itself provides clues regarding the nature and appropriate application – that is, research on African and African-oriented dances and body movements – for the paradigm and methodology.

Age grade See rite of passage.

Amazigh An ethnic group that has resided in Morocco and other locations of North Africa for thousands of years.

Appropriation The act of utilizing or performing another's works, productions, art, culture, and so on, presenting it as one's own, and not obtaining permission from the true creators, and/or not giving credit to the actual progenitors as the creators of the work.

Auxiliary body movements Body movements that are added to root steps for emphasis and creativity. Auxiliary body movements contribute to the overall message that a dance conveys.

Quick reference glossary 49

Balafon Similar to a wooden xylophone, the balafon is comprised of long wooden keys that are affixed to a wooden frame primarily with a material comparable to raffia – a plant in the grass family. Calabashes of diverse sizes are hung underneath the keys to magnify the sound. The wooden keys are arranged in size successively from small to large. Two mallets are utilized to play the balafon, and the size differences of the keys facilitate its ability to produce different tones, notes, and pitches.

Basic step Basic steps are comprised of simple body movements and usually only display three or four body movements.

Body movement The most rudimentary movements of the body – for example, the singular movement of the head in a forward direction or lifting the right leg at any height.

Bomba An African diaspora dance that the African descent population of the island of Puerto Rico performs and passes down through communities and generations.

Bombero A musician that masters playing the bomba drum.

Buleador A drum that keeps the constant rhythm in the bomba dance. It sets the pace for the dance and assures that the pace is maintained throughout.

Characteristically African body movements African dance movements that are referred to as characteristically African contain body movements that are not specific to an African region or ethnicity, but are performed throughout and witnessed in diverse locations on the continent of Africa.

Complex step Multifaceted or multilayered steps that contain body movements that fall outside of the general rudimentary movements usually witnessed within basic steps.

Contraction The forward and backward movements of the torso and/or the pelvic region of the body. A contraction does not include movements from side to side, or circular movements.

Cultural diffusion Cultural diffusion exists when elements of the dance system or when body movements from one culture or ethnic group are spread to and executed by another.

Dance A dance is comprised of a series of curated steps woven together to tell a story.

Dance step A dance step is comprised of two or more body movements executed together or in a sequence or pattern. For instance, the movement of the head forward while lifting the right leg would be considered a step.

Dance system The dance system is all of the elements necessary for the narrative of the Africana dance to be effectively conveyed. Drums and the musicians playing them, dancers and the attire they and the drummers are wearing, the location of the dance performance, the actual dance itself, props, the time of day the dance in executed, and so on are part of the dance system.

Dancer–Drummer Bond The process whereby the drummer accents the dancer's body movements with drum beats and improvised rhythms.

Derdeba See lila.
Djembefola A musician that has mastered playing the djembe drum.
El Seguidor See Primo.
False step A false step is executed by appearing to place the foot on one area of the floor and just before the foot touches the floor, the dancer unexpectedly places the foot somewhere else.
False fall False falls are executed when the dancer appears to trip over their foot and acts as though they are about to fall but gains composure at the last moment before they actually reach the ground.
Fez A felt cylindrical hat with a black tassel attached to the top.
Ganga See Tbel.
Gimbri The gimbri is an instrument traditionally played by the Gnawa. It is a lute with three strings and is played by plucking.
Gnawa An ethic group located in Morocco, Libya, and other locations in Northwestern Africa. The Gnawa were forcibly transported to North Africa via the trans-Saharan slave trade centuries ago. The Gnawa originated in countries in the Western Sahel and south of the Sahara Desert including, Mali, Guinea, Senegal, Gambia, and Guinea Bissau, among others. The predominant ethnic groups among the Gnawa are Mandinka (Mandingo), Fulani, Wolof, Serer, Susu, Bambara, Hausa, among others.
Hajuj See Gimbri
Haratin One of the ethnic groups that are indigenous to Morocco and other parts of Northwestern Africa.
Jali/Jeli A poet, historian, and singer responsible for memorizing several generations and often centuries of historical knowledge. The jali conveys the information via spoken word, chanting, song, dance, with the accompaniment of music. The differences in the spelling of the word jali represent regional variations in pronunciation.
Jola This is, also known as Ajamat, an ethnic group located in Senegal, The Gambia, and Guinea-Bissau, West Africa.
Karkab See Qraqeb.
Lila A spiritual ceremony practiced by the Gnawa ethnic group and occurs at shrines or in private homes. Attendance is by invitation only.
Location-specific body movements Body movements practiced in specific areas of Africa that may not be witnessed in other locations across the continent but are nonetheless undeniably African.
Mandingo See Mandinka.
Mandinka A West African ethnic group primarily located in Western Sahelian territories including Mali, Guinea, Senegal, Gambia, among others. The Mandinka are the progenitors of the historic Mali Empire.
Movement vocabulary The movement vocabulary of a dance is the specific steps that tell the story.

Muqadma This is, also known as the shawafa, a shaman who can communicate with the saints.

Incomplete contractions A body movement that involves the forward or backward thrust of the chest or pelvic region without an equal thrust in the opposite direction. It is distinct from a semi-contraction.

Natural body movements The movements and dance steps that emulate stances and positions that the body naturally performs during daily tasks. Natural body movements also include body movements and dance steps exhibited through gestures naturally displayed consciously and/or subconsciously.

Ngoma In the Central and West Central African language Kikongo, the word "ngoma" is used to denote specific dances, events, and rhythms. In Swahili, a language spoken in East, Central, and Central East Africa, ngoma describes the drums, the dance, and the music.

Pause Pauses are elements of certain complex dance steps that contain a halt or a sometimes barely discernable freeze in movement while executing the step.

Pelvis The area of the body that is located directly under the torso and under the waist. It includes the hips and end where the legs are connected to the hip bones. This area of the body is also known as the pelvic region.

Polyrhythmic body movements Polyrhythmic body movements are performed by moving different parts of the body with two or more rhythmic patterns simultaneously.

Primo A lead drum played during the Afro-Puerto Rican dance, bomba. The primo drummer follows the dancer and accents the steps the dancer is executing.

Qraqeb Also known as krakeb and karkaba, is a musical instrument similar to a castanet and is played by dancers and musicians of the Gnawa ethnic group. The qraqebs are played in pairs, one in each hand.

Rite of passage A process that, historically, all members of the society were required to experience to learn society's laws, customs, and how to be productive members of the society. As a result of Westernization and Globalization, many African societies no longer require the process for adulthood. Alternatively, some African societies have altered the rite of passage process to assure its continuance but to also be compliant with present cultural practices.

Root step The original dance step or original series of body movements, devised before all others in a particular dance.

Semi contractions Partial forward and backward movements of the torso, pelvis, or both simultaneously. Semi-contractions involve equal forward and backward movements of the pelvis or torso regardless of how small the movement may appear. A forward or backward movement of the torso or pelvis without an equal thrust in the opposite direction is an incomplete contraction and should not be confused with a semi- or partial contraction.

Sintir   See gimbri.

Shawafa   See muqadma.

Spectator-dancer   The term spectator-dancer, coined by the author, describes the cyclical actions of audience members who watch the dance as a spectator, and then enters the dance as a performer, and ends the interaction by returning to the audience as a spectator once again. Many traditional secular dances performed in the Western Sahelian region of West Africa – Guinea, Mali, Senegal, Gambia, Guinea-Bissau – encourage spectator-dancer interactions.

Syncopated body movements   Syncopated body movements are witnessed when steps that would normally be subtle or recessive, are accented and brought to a prominent position. These steps are usually executed in unexpected spaces in the dance.

Syncretism   In dance, syncretism exists when separate dance system elements or body movements from different ethnic groups, cultures, or areas of the world are combined to create a new dance or dance system.

Trans-Saharan slave trade   The trans-Saharan slave trade was the trade of enslaved Africans from locations south of the Sahara Desert to locations in North Africa, and the Persian Gulf, also known as the Arab world.

Tbel   A drum with a skin attached to both sides. It is played with one straight stick and one curved stick. The drummer observes the dancer and plays accents on the drum to accentuate the dancer's body movements.

Torso   The part of the body that is located in the upper region of the body between the armpits and the lower part of the waist above the hips. It houses the ribcage and subsequently the lungs.

Tuareg   A seminomadic African ethnic group that practices Islam and primarily resides in the Sahara Desert.

Wolof   The Wolof are a West African ethnic group that primarily reside in Southern Mauritania, Senegal, and Gambia.

Bibliography

Abiola, Ofosuwa. *History Dances: Chronicling the History of Traditional Mandinka Dance*. London: Routledge, 2019.
———. *Fire Under My Feet: History, Race, and Agency in African Diaspora Dance*. London: Routledge, 2022.
Adair, Christy, and Ramsay Burt, eds. *British Dance: Black Routes*. London: Routledge, 2017.
Ajayi, Omofolabo S. *Yoruba Dance: The Semiotics of Movement and Body Attitude in a Nigerian Culture*. Trenton: Africa World Press Inc., 1998.
Alamo-Pastrana, Carlos. "Con El Eco De Los Barriles: Race, Gender and The Bomba Imaginary in Puerto Rico." *Identities* 16, no. 5 (2009): 573–600. https://www.tandfonline.com/doi/abs/10.1080/10702890903172736.
Ali, Omar H. *The World in a Life, Malik Ambar: Power and Slavery Across the Indian Ocean*. Oxford: Oxford University Press, 2016.
Asante, Molefi Kete, and Abu S. Abarry, eds. *African Intellectual Heritage: A Book of Sources*. Philadelphia: Temple University Press, 1996.
Banham, Martin, ed. *A History of Theatre in Africa*. Cambridge: Cambridge University Press, 2004.
Barry, Boubacar. *Senegambia and the Atlantic Slave Trade*. Cambridge: Cambridge University Press, 1998.
Becker, Cynthia. "Sufis, Soldiers, and Minstrels: The Diaspora Aesthetics of the Moroccan Gnawa." *Anthropology and Aesthetics*, no. 59/60 (Spring-Autumn 2011): 124–44.
———. *Blackness in Morocco: Gnawa Identity Through Music and Visual Culture*. Minneapolis: University of Minnesota Press, 2020.
Beckwith, Carol, and Angela Fisher. *Faces of Africa: Thirty Years of Photography*. District of Columbia: National Geographic, 2004.
Belcher, Stephen. *African Myths of Origin*. New York: Penguin Books, 2005.
Borrows, John, and Kent McNeil, eds. *Voicing Identity: Cultural Appropriation and Indigenous Issues*. Toronto: University of Toronto Press, 2022.
Bracey Jr., John H., Sonia Sanchez, and James Smethurst, eds. *SOS – Calling All Black People: A Black Arts Movement Reader*. Amherst: University of Massachusetts Press, 2014.
Burrows, Cedric D. *Rhetorical Crossover: The Black Presence in White Culture*. Pittsburg: University of Pittsburg Press, 2020.
Butt-Thompson, F.W. *West African Secret Societies*. London: H.F. & G. Witherby, 1929.

Bibliography

Cartagena, Juan. "When Bomba Becomes the National Music of the Puerto Rican Nation . . . ." *Centro Journal* XVI, no. 1 (2004): 14–35. https://www.redalyc.org/articulo.oa?id=37716103.

Carter, Donald Martin. *Navigating the African Diaspora: The Anthropology of Invisibility.* Minneapolis: University of Minnesota Press, 2010.

Chernoff, John Miller. *African Rhythm and African Sensibility: Aesthetics and Social Action in African Musical Idioms.* Chicago: University of Chicago Press, 1979.

Collins, Peter, and Anselma Gallinat, eds. *The Ethnographic Self as Resource: Writing Memory and Experience into Ethnography.* New York: Berghahn Books, 2010.

Dagan, Esther A., ed. *The Spirit's Dance in Africa: Evolution, Transformation and Continuity in Sub-Sahara.* Quebec: Galerie Amrad African Arts Publications, 1997.

Daniel, Yvonne. *Dancing Wisdom: Embodied Knowledge in Haitian Vodou, Cuban Yoruba, and Bahian Candomblé.* Urbana: University of Illinois Press, 2005.

Das, Joanna Dee. *Katherine Dunham: Dance and the African Diaspora.* New York: Oxford University Press, 2017.

Drewal, Margaret Thompson. *Yoruba Ritual: Performers, Play, Agency.* Bloomington: Indiana University Press, 1992.

Ebron, Paulla A. *Performing Africa.* Princeton: Princeton University Press, 2002.

El Hamel, Chouki. *Black Morocco: A History of Slavery, Race, and Islam.* Cambridge: Cambridge University Press, 2013.

Ephirim-Donkor, Anthony. *African Personality and Spirituality: The Role of Abosom and Human Essence.* Lanham: Lexington Books, 2016.

Falola, Toyin, and Matt D. Childs, eds. *The Yoruba Diaspora in the Atlantic World.* Bloomington: Indiana University Press, 2004.

Friedson, Steven M. *Dancing Prophets: Musical Experience in Tumbuka Healing.* Chicago: University of Chicago Press, 1996.

Fuhrer, Margaret. *American Dance: The Complete Illustrated History.* Minneapolis: Voyageur Press, 2014.

Fu-Kiau, Kimbwandende K.B. *African Cosmology of the Bantu-Kongo: Principles of Life & Living.* Middletown: African Tree Press, 2001.

Gorer, Geoffrey. *Africa Dances.* London: Elan, 1962.

Gottschild, Brenda Dixon. *Digging the Africanist Presence in American Performance: Dance and Other Contexts.* Westport: Praeger, 1996.

———. *The Black Dancing Body: A Geography From Coon to Cool.* New York: Palgrave Macmillan, 2003.

Guillen, Fuster, and Doris Elida. "Qualitative Research: Hermeneutical Phenomenological Method." *Propósitos y Representaciones* 7, no. 1 (January-April 2019). https://files.eric.ed.gov/fulltext/EJ1212514.pdf.

Hall, Gwendolyn Midlo. *Slavery and African Ethnicities in the Americas: Restoring the Links.* Chapel Hill: University of North Carolina Press, 2005.

Hamdun, Said, and Noel King. *Ibn Battuta in Black Africa.* Princeton: Markus Wiener Publishers, 2010.

Heywood, Linda M., ed. *Central Africans and Cultural Transformations in the American Diaspora.* Cambridge: Cambridge University Press, 2002.

Holloway, Joseph E. *Africanisms in American Culture.* Bloomington: Indiana University Press, 2005.

Huet, Michael. *The Dance, Art and Ritual of Africa.* New York: Patheon Books, 1976.

———. *The Dances of Africa.* London: Thames and Hudson Ltd., 1996.

Jackson, Lauren Michele. *White Negroes: When Cornrows Were in Vogue . . . and Other Appropriation*. Boston: Beacon Press, 2019.

Kawamura, Yoniya, and Jung-Whan Marc de Jong, eds. *Cultural Appropriation in Fashion and Entertainment*. London: Bloomsbury Visual Arts, 2022.

King, Rodreguez-Dorset. *Black Dance in London, 1730–1850: Innovation, Tradition and Resistance*. Jefferson: McFarland & Company Inc., Publishers, 2008.

Knowles, Mark. *Tap Roots: The Early History of Tap Dancing*. Jefferson: McFarland & Company, Inc., Publishers, 2002.

Korbrenski, Dave. *Djoliba Crossing: Journeys Into West African Music and Culture*. New Hampshire: Artemisia Books, 2020.

Lang'ete, Nice. *The Girls in the Wild Fig Tree: How I Fought to Save Myself, My Sister, and Thousands of Girls Worldwide*. New York: Little, Brown and Company, 2021.

Leavy, Patricia. *Essentials of Transdisciplinary Research: Using Problem-Centered Methodologies*. London: Routledge, 2016.

Mark, Peter. *The Wild Bull and the Sacred Forest: Form, Meaning and Change in Senegambian Initiation Masks*. Cambridge: Cambridge University Press, 1992.

Mbiti, John S. *Introduction to African Religion*. 2nd ed. Long Grove: Waveland Press, Inc., 1991.

McAnany, Emile G. *Saving the World: A Brief history of Communication for Development and Social Change*. Urbana: University of Illinois Press, 2021.

McNaughton, Patrick R. *A Bird Dance Near Saturday City: Sisi Ballo and the Art of West African Masquerade*. Bloomington: Indiana University Press, 2008.

Meshesha, Million, and C.V. Jawahar. "Indigenous Scripts of African Languages." *Indilinga African Journal of Indigenous Knowledge Systems* 6, no. 2 (May 15, 2007).

Nii-Yartey, Francis. *African Dance in Ghana: Contemporary Transformations*. London: Mot Juste Limited, 2016.

Nzegwu, Nkiru, ed. *A Companion to African Philosophy*. Malden: Blackwell Publishing Ltd., 2004.

Palacio, Joseph O., ed. *The Garifuna A Nation Across Borders: Essays in Social Anthropology*. Benque Viejo del Carmen, Belize: Cubola Books, 2005.

Reinaldo, Román L. "Scandalous Race: Garveyism, the Bomba, and the Discourse of Blackness in 1920s Puerto Rico." *Caribbean Studies* 31, no. 1 (2003): 213–59. http://www.jstor.org/stable/25613394.

Reynolds, Dee, and Matthew Reason. *Kinesthetic Empathy in Creative and Cultural Practices*. Bristol: Intellect, 2012.

Rockie, Simon. *Death and the Invisible Powers: The World of Kongo Belief*. Bloomington: Indiana University Press, 1993.

Schwartz, Peggy, and Murray Schwartz. *The Dance Claimed Me: A Biography of Pearl Primus*. New Haven: Yale University Press, 2011.

Skaine, Rosemarie. *Female Genital Mutilation: Legal, Cultural and Medical Issues*. Jefferson: McFarland & Company Inc., Publishers, 2005.

Sloat, Susanna, ed. *Caribbean Dance: From Abakua to Zouk: How Movement Shapes Identity*. Gainesville: University of Florida Press, 2002.

———. *Making Caribbean Dance: Continuity and Creativity in Island Cultures*. Gainesville: University Press of Florida, 2010.

Smith, Linda Tuhiwai. *Decolonizing Methodologies: Research and Indigenous Peoples*. London: Bloomsbury Publishing, 2021.

Stearns, Marshall, and Jean Stearns. *Jazz Dance: The Story of American Vernacular Dance*. New York: Da Capo Press, 1994.

Sum, Maisie. "Staging the Sacred: Musical Structure and Processes of the Gnawa Lila in Morocco." *Ethnomusicology* 55, no. 1 (Winter 2011): 77–111. https://www.jstor.org/stable/10.5406/ethnomusicology.55.1.0077.

———. "Music for the Unseen: Interaction Between Two Realms During a Gnawa Lila." *African Music* 9, no. 3 (2013): 151–82. https://www.jstor.org/stable/24877319.

Thompson, Alister. "Four Paradigm Transformations in Oral History." *The Oral History Review* 34, no. 1 (Winter-Spring 2007): 49.

Thompson, Robert Farris. *Flash of the Spirit: African & Afro-American Art & Philosophy*. New York: Vintage Books, 1983.

Tiérou, Alphonse. *Dooplé: The Eternal Law of African Dance*. New York: Routledge, 1992.

Welsh Asante, Kariamu, ed. *African Dance: An Artistic, Historical and Philosophical Inquiry*. Trenton: Africa World Press, Inc., 1994.

Weston, Randy. *The African Aesthetic: Keeper of the Traditions*. Westport: Praeger, 1993.

———. *African Rhythms: The Autobiography of Randy Weston (Refiguring American Music)*. Durham: Duke University Press, 2010.

Williams, Justin A., ed. *The Cambridge Companion to Hip-Hop*. Cambridge: Cambridge University Press, 2015.

Wiredu, Kwesi, ed. *A Companion to African Philosophy*. Malden: Blackwell Publishing, 2004.

Witulski, Christopher. "Contentious Spectacle: Negotiated Authenticity within Morocco's Gnawa Ritual." *Ethnomusicology* 62, no. 1 (Winter 2018): 58–82. https://www.jstor.org/stable/10.5406/ethnomusicology.62.1.0058.

Young, Jason R. *Rituals of Resistance: African Atlantic Religion in Kongo and the Lowcountry South in the Era of Slavery*. Baton Rouge: Louisiana State University, 2007.

Video recordings

The 50 Years Golden "Jubilee". Les Ballets Africains. DVD. 2004; McFarland & Company Inc., Publishers, WI: World Music Productions.

Heritage. Les Ballets Africains. DVD. 1996; Brisbane, Australia: Large Scale Productions, 2007.

Kooyinma. Les Ballet Bagata in Concert. DVD. Directed by Youssouf Koumbassa. 1996; New York, NY: Yousouf Koumbassa + B-Rave Studio, 1996.

Index

Abosom 34
Acogny, Germaine 2
acute torso 19–20, 26, 27, 29, 48
African aesthetic 2–3, 9, 12–14, 30, 36, 48; African dance aesthetic 1, 12–14, 24, 30, 37, 42
Afrikinesis 1, 3–5, 7–8, 9, 10n1, 12–14, 26, 29–34, 36–8, 42–3, 48
Akan 34, 39n11
Amazigh 32, 48
appropriation 7–8, 43, 48

balafon 5, 41, 46, 49
bomba 31–2, 38, 51
bombero 32, 49
buleador 32, 49

characteristically African 2–3, 13–14, 19, 24–5, 27, 29–30, 33, 37
colonization 4, 33, 35
contraction 23–4, 49; incomplete contraction 51–2; partial contraction 29; pelvic contraction 14, 24, 27; semi contraction 51; torso 21–5, 27, 31
cowrie shells 34, 39n12
cultural diffusion 14–15, 49
culture 3–8, 9, 11–16, 26–9, 31–3, 35, 37, 41–3, 48–9

dancer-drummer bond 31, 33–4, 49
Daniel, Yvonne 12
djembe 15, 32, 50
djembefola 32, 50
Dunham, Katherine 2
dununba 36–8

enslavement 4, 35
ethnocentric 5–6
Eurocentric 4–7

Garifuna 16
Gnawa 32–5, 50–1
griot 5–6

Haratin 32, 38n5, 50

Ibn Battuta 5–6
interpretivism 2

jali 5, 41–3, 44n1, 50
Jola 42, 44n5, 50
juba 7

lila 34–5, 50
lived experiences 2–4, 7, 11, 13–14, 29, 30, 32, 37, 43, 48
location-specific movements 13, 25–26, 31, 33–4, 37, 50

Mandinka 5–6, 15, 31–2, 34, 36, 42, 50
memory 3–4; collective 4
minstrelsy 7
Morocco 33–5, 48, 50
movement 1, 7, 9, 13–14, 18, 20–7, 29, 31–3, 37–8, 42, 46, 48–51; auxiliary body movements 19, 48; body movements 1–3, 5, 7–9, 13–15, 18–19, 23–7, 29–33, 36–8, 42–3, 45, 48–52; movement vocabulary 1, 8, 19, 27–28, 31, 37, 50
muqadma 35, 51

natural body movements 26–7, 51
ngoma 15, 31, 51

oral history 3
Orisha 34
orphaned culture 7–8

pause 19, 24, 26, 31, 44n4, 51
pelvis 24, 51
plantations 7
polyrhythmic body movements 25–6, 51
positivism 2
primo 32, 51

qraqeb 33, 51

rite of passage 12, 35–6, 46–7, 48, 51

Sahel 32, 34, 36, 38n6, 50
Senegambia 31, 36, 42
Slave Code 6
spectator-dancer 45, 47n1, 52
step 3, 7, 13–14, 18–19, 24–9, 31–3, 36–8, 42; basic step 19, 26; complex steps 19, 26, 49, 51; false steps 19, 26, 29, 50; root step 18–19, 36–7, 48, 51; step-dancing 7
Stono Insurrection 6–7
syncopated body movements 26, 29, 52
syncretism 14–16, 32–3, 52
systems 3, 6, 13, 42; cultural 7–9, 34; dance systems 2–3, 8–9, 14–16, 26, 31–4, 36, 43; religious systems 11–12; spiritual systems 34; systems 7–8, 34

tap dance 6–7
tbel 33, 52
trans-Saharan slave trade 32, 35, 39n14, 50, 52
Tuareg 32, 38n5, 52

Umfundalai 2

Welsh, Kariamu 2, 12
western 2–4, 8, 16, 32, 36, 50; Sahel 39n15, 50
Wolof 32, 50, 52

Yoruba 16, 34

For Product Safety Concerns and Information please contact our EU representative GPSR@taylorandfrancis.com
Taylor & Francis Verlag GmbH, Kaufingerstraße 24, 80331 München, Germany

www.ingramcontent.com/pod-product-compliance
Lightning Source LLC
Chambersburg PA
CBHW051800230426
43670CB00012B/2372